KU-731-163

1205
ADV

SOCIAL STUDIES
LIBRARY
SOCIAL STUDIES CENTRE, GEORGE ST.
OXFORD. OX1 2RL

WITHDRAWN

SOCIAL STUDIES
LIBRARY.
45, WELLINGTON SQUARE,
OXFORD.

WITHDRAWN

WITHDRAWN

WITHDRAWN

WITHDRAWN

ADVANCED URBAN TRANSPORT

Advanced Urban Transport

41557

Ian BLACK, Richard GILLIE,
Richard HENDERSON and Terry THOMAS

Urban Transport Research Group
University of Warwick

SOCIAL STUDIES
LIBRARY,
S, WELLINGTON SQUARE,
OXFORD.

SOCIAL STUDIES
LIBRARY
SOCIAL STUDIES CENTRE, GEORGE ST
OXFORD. OX1 2RL

WITHDRAWN

SAXON HOUSE | LEXINGTON BOOKS

©Ian Black, Richard Gillie, Richard Henderson and Terry Thomas, 1975

All rights reserved. No part of this publication may be reproduced, stored in a retrieval system, or transmitted in any form or by any means, electronic, mechanical, photo-copying, recording, or otherwise without the prior permission of D. C. Heath Ltd.

Published by

SAXON HOUSE, D. C. Heath Ltd.
Westmead, Farnborough, Hants., England.

Jointly with

LEXINGTON BOOKS, D. C. Heath & Co.
Lexington, Mass. USA.

.

ISBN 0 347 01081 4
Library of Congress Catalog Card Number 75-3834

Printed in Great Britain
by Unwin Brothers Limited
The Gresham Press, Old Woking, Surrey
A member of the Staples Printing Group

Contents

List of figures

List of tables

Preface

In 1972, the (British) Science Research Council awarded a grant to the Urban Transport Research Group of Warwick University 'to assess the feasibility and desirability of introducing small, reserved-route public transport systems into towns'. This book presents some of the findings of the resultant research. It is intended as a general text for those professionally concerned with the design, assessment or operation of such systems.

During the course of the research, many colleagues assisted the authors. Special thanks are extended to David Turner, who initiated the research proposal to the SRC and has been involved in the subject since 1964. Important contributions were made by Chris Longley and Howard Riley, who were both full-time members of the group, and by Brian Styles and Bill Ogden of Lanchester Polytechnic, who were members of its steering committee. Numerous outside specialists have been consulted by the authors; among the most helpful were staff of the Coventry Transportation Study Group, who provided much valuable information about the transport scene in the city.

1 Introduction

Urban transport today presents a depressing and bewildering picture. Increasing congestion, noise and air pollution, the emergence of a group of people deprived of adequate transport, and the ever-increasing cost of public transport are some of the more conspicuous features that give cause for concern. The changing direction of public policy in recent years is the product of the extra effort and thought devoted to resolving these problems. However, these changes in policy are only the beginning of a difficult and continuous process of accommodating people's increasing desire for mobility with a comfortable and acceptable urban environment.

This book examines the rôle automated transport might play in our towns and cities, and the form it might take. Our concern with automation should not be interpreted as a belief that it offers a panacea for the problems of urban transport. Far from it − more efficient utilisation of existing transport resources, together with improvements to conventional transport modes, must provide the basis of policy in the forseeable future. Automation can be only a small element in that programme.

The assessment of new technology raises many difficulties. In particular, many ideas now incorporated only in prototypes may perform quite differently in passenger service or may evolve into a quite different form from that currently anticipated. This problem is compounded by the difficulty of accurately foreseeing people's reaction to new modes of operation and the intrusion of new structures into the urban scene.

In our assessment of automated transport we have attempted to maintain a balance between a consideration of the technical details of the new technology and an appraisal of its economic and environmental features. In two senses the assessment might be considered too narrow and parochial. We have concentrated on transport in the United Kingdom and, although we believe many of the conclusions to be relevant to other countries, make only brief references to the particular circumstances found in the USA and Europe. Similarly, some of the techniques used in the economic and environmental appraisal are peculiar to Great Britain and may have only limited relevance to other parts of the world.

In Chapter 2 we examine the forms of public transport that exist in the United Kingdom today and the constraints on their development. This is followed in Chapter 3 by a short review of automated transport. This introduces the next three chapters, which are devoted to the technical details of the vehicles, track, stations and control that make up an automated system. Chapters 7 and 8 assess the economic and environmental influence of possible routes in a particular city (Coventry). This is followed by a discussion of the wider conclusions that can be derived from Coventry. Chapter 10 examines the history of automated transport development and identifies the part played by government policy.

2 The State of Public Transport in British Cities

The historical legacy

The existence of mechanical means of transport in urban areas is a product largely of social changes, and of the technological response to them in the last half of the nineteenth century. Until the 1870s the railway provided the only form of motorised transport, and was primarily concerned with the transport of passengers and goods over long distances. Because of the short duration of most town journeys, coupled with the high cost of providing track, urban railways were confined to the larger cities. 'Metropolitan Railways' designed specifically to cater for urban travel existed in London; and in the larger cities, such as Manchester, the railway companies provided suburban-type passenger services along routes originally provided for what would now be called inter-city services.

Until the 1870s most urban journeys would have been undertaken on foot; however, this was becoming increasingly arduous as towns grew in size, as a response to both an increasing population and a fall in urban densities, brought about partly by the fashion for suburban living, and partly by the increasingly rigorous public health legislation.

Initially, urban transport for the rapidly expanding towns was provided by an adaptation of the railway – the horse tram (with conversion to electric traction at the turn of the century) – but the development of the internal combustion engine opened up the possibility of safe motorised transport that did not require the construction of special tracks and could use existing streets. In the first quarter of the twentieth century, the internal combustion engine proved capable of a wide variety of transport applications: it could be used either in a 'personal' vehicle – a private car or motor-cycle – or in a larger vehicle suitable for dealing with the level of passenger movement previously served by the horse bus.

These four means of catering for passenger travel – the urban railway, the tramway, the bus, and the private vehicle – have provided the basis for passenger movement in urban areas for the rest of the century. Although many improvements in design, together with minor changes in operating philosophy, have been made, these forms have remained

3

basically unchanged. What has changed, however, as people's incomes and tastes have altered, is the relative importance of each mode.

The form of British towns — the location of activities and of the transport corridors serving them — has changed gradually during the twentieth century. Road networks tend to be predominantly radial, although many towns have tried to make circumferential movement easier. In the 1950s and 1960s, the 'inner ring road', the purpose of which was to keep road traffic out of the central area, was an important idea in transport planning. Bus routes and the now-extinct tram routes have also had a strong radial pattern, which has been largely unaffected by the dispersion of employment (though not retail employment) from the town centres.

The existing road network, together with the occasional railway route, is a legacy that limits both the freedom of action available to urban planners and the opportunities for comprehensive redevelopment. Proposals for future development need to take account of this background, with its tendency to favour gradual, rather than dramatic, change.

Basic characteristics of transport modes

The means of catering for passenger movement, produced by technical innovation at the end of the last century, can be classified by a number of key elements, which define their manner of operation. These elements are:

(1)   the type of vehicle — whether it is personal or shared;
(2)   the nature of the right of way — whether it is for the exclusive use of a particular mode or used by other modes and for other purposes;
(3)   the method of guiding the vehicle along the right of way — whether or not the vehicle is captive to the track.

Shared vehicles

There are two reasons why it is more advantageous to use large vehicles, shared by a number of travellers, than to use small private vehicles: first, the financial costs of operation per passenger are smaller; and, secondly, large vehicles can make better use of a right of way.

The economies of operation that accrue to a shared vehicle are illustrated by comparing the average cost of operating a car to the average cost of operating a bus. In 1972, the average cost per unit of capacity was 1·0p per km for a car, and 0·4p per km for a bus.[1] The cost per passenger km depends on the occupancy of the different vehicles.

4

In addition, for a given right of way, more people can be carried in large shared vehicles than in smaller vehicles. Again, a comparison between the bus and private car is instructive: a bus is usually reckoned to be equivalent to three cars in a traffic stream, but may carry up to 20 times as many people; thus, in terms of units of capacity (ignoring load factors), a bus is over six times as economical in its use of road space. It is obvious from this that, when demand approaches or exceeds capacity,[2] the costs of providing a right of way for travel by bus are lower than for providing the same facility for travel by car.

The prime disadvantage of using large shared vehicles is their inferior service. Private vehicles provide an 'on-demand' service tailored to the needs of the individual, whereas the shared vehicle must try to satisfy an average of these demands. This means that many travellers have long walks to a bus stop or station, and have their journey disrupted while the vehicle stops to allow other passengers to board or alight. A 'dial-a-ride' bus service using shared vehicles tries to create a more personal service by providing a door-to-door journey, but without eliminating the stopping element. The only fully personal public service is the taxi. Together these two modes demonstrate that as the service improves the cost rises.

Exclusive rights of way

All towns contain a comprehensive network of rights of way that provide access to property. Usually these provide vehicular access, but in a few cases only pedestrians may use them. These all-purpose channels of communication also fulfil other functions: they may house street markets or shops, act as a meeting place for people and provide wayleaves for public utilities, as well as allow sufficient air and light to reach the adjoining buildings. All these functions may coexist comfortably and efficiently as long as individual demands on the corridor are modest. When the right of way has to cater not only for vehicles wanting access to local property, but also for vehicles passing through *en route* to another destination, serious conflicts begin to arise. Such conflicts are aggravated if the vehicles travel fast, are dangerous, are noisy, or emit unpleasant fumes.

The question of segregation then arises. Segregation may take the simple form of dividing the right of way into pavement and roadway, defining the legal rights of pedestrians and drivers, and restricting other activities along the corridor. If the passage of vehicles is particularly heavy, the possibility of constructing a new segregated route solely for the use of vehicles may be proposed. This route must then be justified on the basis of the improvement in service it provides or the improvement in the conditions of the right of way it partially replaces, or a combination of both. The justification may be provided by the ability of the segregated way to pay its way financially or to satisfy wider public-service arguments.

Exclusive rights of way may take various forms: the railways and, to a lesser extent, the tram use rights of way that exclude other vehicles and pedestrians; motorways and bus-ways are the most restricted forms used by motor vehicles, although other forms may provide partial restriction.

Even though through traffic in an urban street may make a reserved way desirable, it is only in areas where passenger demand is high that this can be justified. Thus, only in larger towns are urban railways found. Exclusive tram rights of way were once to be found in medium-sized British towns (population 300,000 to 1 million). In the last 20 years, the increasing demand for travel by private vehicle has resulted in numerous proposals for urban motorways in towns with a population greater than 300,000. Much effort has been devoted to estimating the thresholds of passenger demand that justify an exclusive right of way. The magic figure of 1 million is often suggested as the minimum population necessary to justify the construction of an urban railway, but individual circumstances will lead to different answers. The cost or difficulty of constructing a new route, the pattern of demand in the city and the alternative transport available will all influence the decision. If a reserved right of way already exists, the threshold of demand necessary to keep the route open will be much lower, since the construction cost has already been suffered and need not enter the calculations.

Captive vehicles

By a 'captive' vehicle we mean one whose path is rigorously defined by the track upon which it operates. The railway and the tram provide classic examples.

The advantage of captive vehicles is twofold. First, it is possible, due to the well-defined path they follow, to use more compact rights of way. This is particularly important where there is extensive tunnelling (cost increases rapidly with the bore diameter of a tunnel) and where there are such restrictions as bridges along the right of way.[3] Secondly, articulated vehicles − and hence high-capacity vehicles − can more easily be used when the vehicle is captive. It has been argued,[4] in the context of railways and buses, that this is an illusory advantage and that buses operating on a segregated route could provide a similar capacity to an urban railway. This may be true along open track, but the difficulty, with small vehicles, of loading and unloading substantial flows of passengers at stations means that the larger-capacity rail vehicle retains its advantage.

Although captive vehicles do not necessarily need an exclusive right of way, their method of operation often means that they cannot be successfully integrated with other modes or activities; for example, in cases where platforms or stations are large, where high speed (often accompanied by poor braking ability) is desirable, or where the track is incompatible with other functions. The railway demonstrates these three features, but the tram — by means of a track flush to the roadway, modest stations, and low speeds — was successfully adapted to a shared right of way. A mode that requires an exclusive right of way at all times has the distinct disadvantage of being unable to use an existing right of way where demand is low — in the suburban areas of a town, for instance. Similarly, a captive vehicle, although it may not need an exclusive right of way, needs an exclusive track.

Trends in the demand for transport

At the beginning of the 1950s, most passenger travel demand was satisfied by means of the facilities provided by public transport operators. In 1952, 38,000 million passenger km were travelled on the railways, 80,000 million on public service vehicles (buses, coaches and trams), and 61,000 million by private car. The next 20 years saw a period of rapid change in people's travel behaviour. The increase in the demand for passenger travel was satisfied mainly by the use of the private car. Indeed, the use of public transport was in decline not merely relative to the total quantity of travel, but in absolute terms as well. The trends are illustrated in Fig. 2.1, and Table 2.1 shows the rate of change in travel by different modes for the two decades 1952–62 and 1962–72.

Table 2.1

Passenger movement by different modes:
per cent rate of change per annum

	All modes	Private vehicles	Public service vehicles	Rail
1952–62	4·4	10·9	−1·8	−0·6
1962–72	4·9	7·6	−1·9	−0·8

Source: *Passenger Transport in Great Britain*, 1972.

7

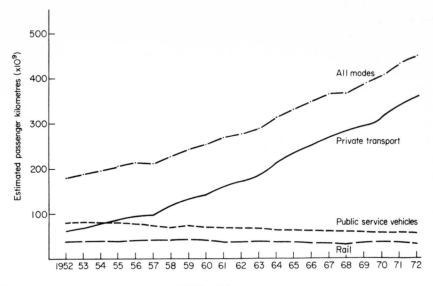

Fig. 2.1 Passenger movement, 1952–72
Source: *Passenger Transport in Great Britain, 1972*

The major cause of this change in the pattern of demand was the rapid growth in car ownership (8.4 per cent a year), itself a result of the continuous rise in real incomes during the post-war period. Households purchasing a car for the first time naturally transferred most of their journeys from public to private transport. The new opportunities opened up by car ownership and its low marginal cost meant many extra (and longer) trips were made. This tendency to substitute private for public transport was reinforced by a number of factors – in particular, the decline in the service offered by public transport and the deterioration in its relative price level.

A public transport operator faced with a fall in demand (and the need to meet costs out of revenue) can either cut costs by reducing the frequency of the service he offers, or increase revenue by raising fares. Both moves are likely to lead to a further reduction in passenger demand. Regression analysis of urban bus operation suggests that a 1 per cent increase in fares might reduce demand by 0·3 per cent, and a 1 per cent decrease in vehicle km might reduce demand by 0·7 per cent.[5] Public transport operators faced with this choice generally choose a combination of both options. In the main urban areas, a 52 per cent fall in passenger journeys during the period 1952–72 was accompanied by a fall of 31 per cent in vehicle km.[6]

If we look at the price position of public transport, relative to the price of 'all goods and services' as well as private transport, we find a deterioration much greater than we would expect from a simple reaction to falling passenger demand. Fig. 2.2 describes the trend. This shows that, during the 1950s and 1960s, the price of travel by public transport has increased more rapidly than the cost of other goods and services (all the indices in Fig. 2.2 are deflated by the price index for all consumers' expenditure), whereas the price of motor vehicles and their operation has fallen. The movement towards one-man operation of buses (this began in the mid-1960s) has provided only a modest, and temporary, respite from the remorseless increase in costs (partly, it must be admitted, at the expense of the quality of service provided). However, public authorities have shown a greater willingness, during the 1970s, to subsidise fares, and this may change future trends. The rise in the price of petrol during late 1973 and 1974 has significantly increased the cost of motoring. It is too early to say whether these factors will provide merely a temporary relief to public transport or herald the beginning of more favourable trends.

Other factors in the last two decades have reduced the level of service offered to the public transport passenger. Operators have claimed that traffic management schemes, while benefiting the private car, have made

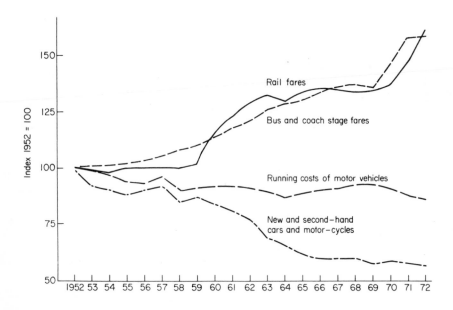

Fig. 2.2   Transport price indices, 1952–72
Note: all indices are deflated by the index for total consumers' expenditure

bus services less convenient to the passenger. Route distance has been increased by one-way systems without any compensating increase in passenger demand, and such schemes have also made route systems complicated and difficult for the passenger to understand; in addition, pedestrian precincts have denied the operator direct access to town centres. Finally, it has been alleged, congestion has increased the variability of running times, and thus increased the unreliability of bus services.

Transport planning: the rôle of public authorities

The intervention of governments in the process of transport investment has a long history. As far as public transport is concerned, much of the traditional justification for intervention has been based on the need to restrain the exercise of monopoly powers. Thus railways, and to a lesser extent canals, were, from their inception, subject to stringent government regulation, but this did not seem an embarrassment to nineteenth-century governments otherwise committed to faith in *laissez-faire*. It was clear even then that transport investment impinged on so many spheres of life that the financial costs of a project would not necessarily reflect its true costs — or benefits — to the community. For instance, the construction and maintenance of roads has been traditionally a public responsibility, the criterion for road investment being based on 'need' — that is, that roads should be maintained (by local authorities) in such a state as to accommodate the traffic wishing to use them. This was satisfactory in situations where there was no great growth in road transport, and where most traffic was local — a cost imposed by local residents and met out of local rates. But the growth in long-distance transport in the eighteenth century could not be accommodated by such procedures, and thus the government tried to impose the cost of road improvements and maintenance on the road user, by permitting the formation of turnpike trusts, which were responsible for collecting tolls. The experiment was not very successful, but the consequences of failure were avoided by the emergence of canal and rail transport, after which roads resumed their former rôle as local arteries of communication maintained for the benefit of all at local expense.

Legislation was designed to cope with the rapid expansion of public transport facilities — first of the railways and then of the bus industry. The main purpose of the legislation was to ensure an orderly extension of routes without unnecessary duplication, while at the same time ensuring

10

that the resultant monopoly powers were not misused.

The problems that the turnpike trusts had failed to solve were to reoccur in the twentieth century, with the revival of road transport. This time the public authorities eschewed the turnpike solution. Initially a Road Fund was set up, collecting revenue from car owners and using the proceeds to provide roads with a surface more suited to motor traffic. The idea of an hypothecated tax on motor vehicles was abandoned in the 1920s and the old needs formula readopted (though reapportioning some responsibility from local to central government). Thus, if more traffic caused bigger potholes, then more money must be spent on filling them up; and, if a road were too narrow for the increased traffic, then it must be widened or rebuilt. With a modest level of car ownership and spare capacity on nearly all roads, the 'needs' were generally small and not an undue burden on the public purse; but, as traffic increased, the 'needs' became more pressing.

The report *Traffic in Towns,*[7] published in 1963 and better known as the Buchanan Report, represents one of the last official attempts to apply the needs formula to the problems of accommodating road traffic. The working party saw the problem as a conflict between 'accessibility' and 'environment'. Improvements in accessibility were regarded as a public benefit, most satisfactorily achieved by facilities to permit extensive penetration of urban areas by the car. However, such penetration was not to be achieved at the expense of environmental factors — the pleasure obtained from other public uses of urban streets and spaces — or of major changes in urban form. Unfortunately, the report was unable to show that the needs formula could be reconciled with the environmental and urban-form objectives that the working party had established. In their study of Norwich, a town of only just over 100,000 inhabitants, they concluded that extensive vehicular penetration of the central area would be impossible if environmental objectives were to be satisfied; while, in their studies of Leeds and London, extensive penetration of large areas of these cities was shown to be a physical impossibility, regardless of environmental consequences. The publication of the Buchanan Report highlighted, perhaps unwittingly, the shortcomings of the needs formula. Although the point was not made in the report itself, it was clear that the benefits to be derived from accommodating the car could not justify the considerable costs that such a policy implied.

During the 1960s, it became increasingly apparent that minor road improvements and traffic-management measures would not be able to cope with the anticipated increase in car use, but the Buchanan Report had failed to provide a means of deciding how this problem should be

11

resolved and how much new road construction would be worthwhile. What was needed was some equivalent of the financial rate of return used by public transport operators to decide their investment plans, and this was provided by subjecting proposed road schemes to a limited form of cost-benefit analysis, in which savings in travel time were compared with the capital costs of the scheme. Such an approach was subject to the same limitations as the financial rate of return on public transport investment, since it did not take account of all the costs; but, as a result of this procedure, central government began to get some idea of the amount of investment in new roads that could be justified. Many urban schemes that would have been built under the Buchanan philosophy were shown to be economically unjustified.

In addition, two other arguments were made with increasing vigour. Public inquiries demonstrated the strength of feeling against roads that, while economically justifiable, were open to environmental objections. Consideration of such matters as noise, visual intrusion, air pollution, severance and safety began to appear in (and at times dominate) the appraisal of transport projects. As the service provided by public transport began to decline, it was seen that, even with the rapid rise in car ownership projected, a substantial proportion of the population — notably the elderly, the infirm and the young — would be left without adequate transport if this trend were not halted. The concept of public service began to challenge that of 'revenue should cover cost'. The thinking that developed from the Buchanan Report and the results of early transportation studies (which confirmed the difficulty of accommodating the car) led to the conclusion that there should be a change in the balance between public and private transport if the best use were to be made of the limited resources available to transport. Road pricing, perhaps the ideal solution in theory, was examined in the early 1960s,[8] but was consistently rejected due to the difficulty and expense of imposing charges on motor vehicles in city streets. Parking control became the accepted means of limiting the use of the car for urban journeys, especially commuter travel. The 1968 Transport Act gave some limited financial assistance to public transport. A system of route-specific fare subsidies for railways was introduced and public transport operators could also apply for a 75 per cent grant towards the cost of capital 'infrastructure' (basically buildings and structures) required by their operators. This nominally placed public transport financing on the same basis as road financing (since at this time principal roads were also eligible for a 75 per cent central-government grant), but such grants were of only limited relevance to the bus industry, most of the expenses of which are related to vehicle operation. In addition, the fare subsidies to railways were severely limited in the amount of assistance they gave to public transport in urban areas. The Public Transport Authorities set up in 1968 to co-ordinate the needs of public transport in London and the conurbations helped strengthen the position of public transport by providing a more sympathetic organisational structure.

Emphasis on the rôle public transport should play in long-term urban planning can be seen in the second report of the Expenditure Committee — presented to Parliament in mid-1973[9] — and in the government observations on this report.[10] In particular, the Local Government Act 1972 allowed the local authority, for the first time in urban areas, to support public transport operation with revenue subsidies. The 1972 Act was followed by more detailed proposals for the reorganisation of the arrangements for financing local-authority transport expenditure. In place of the assortment of specific grants for highway construction, new buses, public transport infrastructure, and so on, there is a new system based on a blanket 'Transport Supplementary Grant' (on top of the Rate Support Grant), which may be used for either capital or current expenditure. This, it is hoped, will prevent there being any bias, such as was thought to exist before, towards particular forms of expenditure — especially capital-intensive road schemes. The 'block grant' is made available to a local authority on the presentation of an annual Transport Plan and Programme (TPP) that describes a balanced and comprehensive transport strategy for the area under consideration. Eventually it is intended to reduce the dependence of local authorities on central government supervision by fully incorporating the grant into the Rate Support Grant. The main priority in the interim is to ensure that the TPPs recognise the interaction between the various ingredients of a successful transport policy — road building, revenue support, parking charges, bus priority — and produce a properly balanced and integrated proposal. The last ten years have witnessed a change in the attitude of central and local government towards public transport. The old passive rôle has been rejected, and public transport is now seen as the means by which administrators and engineers hope to resolve the conflicts and stresses engendered by the increasing taste for personal mobility.

Notes

[1] A private car is assumed to have a carrying capacity of four persons. Running costs are estimated at 2·1p per km and annual overhead costs at

£300, spread over 16,000km per annum. These figures are derived from *Schedule of Estimated Running Costs*, Automobile Association, 1973. The *Annual Summary of Accounts and Statistical Information,* published by the Association of Public Passenger Transport Operators, suggests that the cost of operating a bus with a carrying capacity of 80 and covering about 48,000km is about 30p per km.

[2] This qualification derives from the indivisibility of a stretch of road. When demand is low, the cost of providing a road is much the same whether it be for bus or car travel (though the bus may require a slightly wider road and cause higher maintenance costs). Only as demand increases does the choice between a single-lane road for buses and two lanes for cars arise. The deterioration in the level of service due to congestion as demand approaches capacity must also be taken into account in any comparison.

[3] For instance, in the North Tyne study (A.M. Vorhees and Associates, *North Tyne Loop Study,* Tyneside Passenger Transport Executive, 1971) the main argument in favour of light rapid transit compared with a segregated bus-way was the cost of widening long sections of the existing right of way (especially bridges) to cater for the wavering path of a bus operating at 60km per hour or more.

[4] E. Smith, 'An economic comparison of urban railways and express bus services', *Journal of Transport Economics and Policy* vol. 7, no. 1, January 1973. See also reply in *Omnibus Magazine,* July/August 1973, pp. 81–82.

[5] M.G. Smith and P.T. McIntosh, 'Fares elasticity: interpretation and estimation', in *Symposium on Public Transport Fare Structure: Papers and Discussion,* TRRL Supplementary Report 37 UC, Transport and Road Research Laboratory, Crowthorne, Berkshire, 1974.

[6] *Passenger Transport in Great Britain,* HMSO, 1973. The process by which falling passenger demand leads to a fall in the level of service and a rise in fares, which themselves lead to further falls in passengers, is sometimes referred to as a 'vicious spiral' or 'vicious circle'. It should, however, be remembered that the process is finite under most circumstances and can become a 'virtuous circle' if an initial *increase* in demand occurs.

[7] *Traffic in Towns,* HMSO, 1963.

[8] *Road Pricing – the Technical and Economic Possibilities,* Ministry of Transport, HMSO, 1963.

[9] *Urban Transport Planning,* Second Report from the Expenditure Committee, House of Commons, Session 1972–73.

[10] *Urban Transport Planning – Government Observations on the Second Report of the Expenditure Committee,* Cmnd 5366, HMSO, 1973.

3 A Review of Automated Transport

This chapter briefly describes the nature of automated transport systems and some of the arguments advanced in their favour. Later chapters examine these matters in greater detail.

Automation in public transport

Automation is the distinguishing feature of the transport systems that are the subject of this book. The vehicles operating within these systems have no drivers, although the stopping places, or stations, may be manned. Staff would also be needed for the maintenance of vehicles and control equipment, for the cleaning of stations, and for generally overseeing the operation of the system. They may be used in the recovery of broken-down vehicles, perhaps driving them to the nearest station or depot. However, in normal operation the vehicles run under automatic control.

An exact definition of 'automatic control' is not easy. While there exist certain transport systems, such as escalators, that operate continuously without manual supervision, these can be likened to machines: the system cannot react to unexpected demands upon it except by stopping. Automatic control techniques, however, are characterised by their ability to react to unforeseen demands within predetermined limits. If a passenger leaves his umbrella in a vehicle door, a machine might carry on regardless or stop; but an automatic system would, ideally, delay only that vehicle (and others immediately affected by the delay), not the entire system. An automated transport system might also be able to react to changes in passenger demand and to such contingencies as vehicle breakdown.

There is a wide variety of automatic control techniques proposed for automated transport. Some systems are designed to operate with headways of as little as 1 second between vehicles, while others employ a more modest 20 seconds. In comparison, manually controlled urban railways work to a minimum headway of about 90 seconds, whereas cars are frequently driven with headways of less than 1 second. In addition to broad differences of headway, a number of other techniques are being experimented with: marshalling vehicles into trains or platoons when making trips in a common direction; translating vehicles in stations either sideways or vertically in order to make the design of the station simpler; and using computers both to direct vehicles to places on the network with surplus demand, and to modify vehicle schedules according to changes in demand.

Reserved track

It is difficult to contemplate an automated transport system running on a non-segregated route. For the safety of both passengers and non-users, a reserved track that excludes interference with the flow of vehicles must be provided, although it may not always be possible to exclude missiles, or the more determined vandals. The track may be at ground level, in a cutting, on an embankment, underground or overhead. The last has been most widely adopted by developers as the only feasible method of finding routes through urban areas without being faced with the problem of large-scale redevelopment. In addition, route structures may vary in extent, from a simple line haul with no junctions to a city-wide system in which vehicles may travel from any station to any other station over a network. The need for a reserved track at all points on an automated route generates serious environmental problems. All rights of way, from footpaths to motorways, must be crossed by means of a bridge or tunnel; and bridges, or more often viaducts, are particularly difficult to introduce into an existing town in an acceptable manner.

The two alternatives

Two quite different sizes of vehicle are prominent in automated transport. They highlight the different types of service that can be provided, and we refer to them as *autotaxi* and *autotram*. Table 3.1 compares some typical dimensions of the two types with those of trams and urban rail vehicles.

Autotaxi

Autotaxi provides a type of service similar to a road-based taxi. Small automated vehicles, holding between three and six passengers, operate on

16

Table 3.1

Vehicle dimensions of autotaxi, autotram, and two other transport modes

Based on:		Autotaxi Matra 'Aramis'[a]	Autotram LTV 'Airtrans'[b]	Tram VOV[c] recommended standards	Metro
Width	m	1·30	2·13	2·40	2·9–3·1
Height	m	1·90	3·05	3·28	3·55
Length (unit)	m	2·30	6·40	21·30	37·15
Weight	kg	650	6,363	20,000	48,000
Passengers		4	45	115	290
Approximate floor area	m²	2·99	13·63	51·12	111·45
Weight/passenger	kg	162	144	174	166
Weight/floor area	kg/m²	217	467	391	430

[a] Prototype and test track in operation at Orly Airport, Paris.
[b] In revenue operation at Dallas/Fort Worth Airport (USA) since January 1974.
[c] VOV: Verband öffentlicher Verkehrsbetriebe – the West German Association of Public Transport Undertakings.

a network of routes with stations at regular intervals. Intending passengers arrive at a station and board a waiting vehicle, or, if one is not available, an empty vehicle is summoned to the station by a central computer. The passenger, having made his destination known to the central control, is carried there without stopping at intermediate stations. All stations are off-line (i.e. vehicles wishing to stop at a station leave the main line) to ensure that vehicles passing the station are not delayed by stationary ones. The passenger and his associates have exclusive use of a vehicle.

The track network is fully connected and no change of vehicles during a journey is required. Most routes are one-way, to avoid complicated junctions and keep the amount of track in any one street to a minimum. Sophisticated control systems are needed to monitor vehicle movements, and very close headway operation between vehicles is needed to provide sufficient capacity. The vehicles may be adapted to carry goods.

Autotaxi represents a high point in public transport service – a no-waiting, fast, non-stop journey in a personal vehicle. Only in requiring a walk to and from the station does it fail to match the service of the road-based taxi or private car (although, even with these modes, speeds may be low and walks to and from car parks lengthy). Attractive though the service may be to the passenger, the technical difficulties to be overcome and the heavy economic and environmental cost of an autotaxi installation will severely limit its application in the next 10 to 15 years.

Autotram

Autotram provides a service similar in form to that of buses and urban railways. In its simplest form, vehicles travel along one route obeying a fixed schedule and stopping at every station. A number of routes may exist in a town, and for many journeys passengers must change vehicles. The demands on the control system are generally modest compared to autotaxi: headways are rarely less than 10 seconds and routing patterns are usually simple. The vehicles, although small, can generally accommodate seated and standing passengers. Vehicles can also be coupled into short trains to provide more capacity. Routes are generally two-way, with track that is correspondingly bigger than that needed for autotaxi. Conversely, stations are usually small and simple, as vehicles are not continuously overtaking one another.

Variations on a simple stop-everywhere service are possible: some vehicles may not stop at all stations and the schedule may be modified to suit demand. This development necessitates improvements to the control system and more complex station layouts.

Mode names

So far we have referred to two generic types of automated transport — autotaxi and autotram — distinguished by the type of service they provide. Various rather confusing names have arisen for different modes and different systems in this field. A generic classification commonly used in the USA is:

PRT (Personal Rapid Transit)   — autotaxi
GRT (Group Rapid Transit)   ⎫
LGT (Light Guideway Transit)   ⎬ autotram
                                ⎭
LRT (Light Rail Transit)   — trams or 'streetcars'

'Mass Transit' and 'Rapid Transit' usually refer to large capacity urban railways, but are sometimes also used to refer to bus-ways.

When we turn to the names given to systems by manufacturers and developers, we find a plethora of them, among which are included MAT (Mitsubishi Automatic Transportation), KCV (Kawasaki Computer-Controlled Vehicles), and Ford of America's ACT (Automatically Controlled Transportation). It can be seen that acronyms are popular, and the French firm of Matra, manufacturers of the VAL system, managed to find an acronym that describes not only the system *(Véhicules Automatiques Légers),* but also where it was hoped the first installation would be (Villeneuve−d'Ascq−Lille). The firm also seems to be unique in naming its autotaxi system after a literary character − Aramis. One of the four heroes of Dumas' *Three Musketeers,* he was characterised by craftiness, hypocrisy and profound subtlety. Presumably the transport system will attempt to emulate only the last.

Other names chosen by manufacturers are a combination of words or parts of words, as is seen from such names as the self-explanatory 'Cabinentaxi' (the autotaxi system of the German consortium of Demag-MBB) and 'Minitram'. The latter term is used in the UK both as a generic name corresponding to 'autotram' and as the name of the particular system being developed by Hawker Siddeley Dynamics Ltd.

We shall continue to use the terms 'autotaxi' and 'autotram' to distinguish between two quite different types of transport service (associated with the taxi and the tram respectively), while at the same time conveying their automated nature − efficiently, if not elegantly. The term 'metro' will be used to describe an urban railway solely devoted to local passenger transport.

Autotram and the benefits of automation

Many of the ways in which automated transport is claimed to be an improvement on conventional modes are, in part at least, a result of the reserved-track nature of the automated system, and we should beware of attributing all the benefits to automation, though it can be expected that it will lead to some. The replacement of human drivers may mean a cheaper service for passengers, with no deterioration in quality. Alternatively, it may make it possible, without increasing the cost, to introduce improvements in service that were previously out of the question. The actual result will usually be a mixture of reduced cost and improved service. However, all the major protagonists of autotram suggest that automation means more than just a small change grafted onto an existing reserved-track transport system: they argue that automation opens up opportunities that were not available before. In particular, the cost of automatic equipment on the vehicle is likely to be lower than the cost of a human driver (this is not to say that the *total* costs are smaller; costs of static control equipment may be significant), and this encourages the use of smaller vehicles, which can mean a significant reduction in waiting times. Central control of a transport system should also mean better scheduling and superior reaction to sudden changes in passenger demand. Automatic control of vehicles should ensure smoother acceleration profiles and more accurate stopping in stations.

The small cross-section of autotram renders it more acceptable in towns, but it is not specifically an argument in favour of automated trams, since it could quite easily be applied to the design of conventional trams. It may well be that autotram will be successful if it is of small cross-section and operates on a reserved track, but we should avoid arguments that assume that certain components are exclusive to autotram.

4 Track and Stations

Comparative track costs

The support track and stations for autotrams and autotaxis comprise the major part of the capital cost of a system. Although track can be at ground level or underground, most development of automated systems has assumed that the track will be elevated and usually built above streets. This assumption influences the form of the vehicles and the service that can be offered: for example, the desirable minimum turning radius of the vehicle is determined by the space available at street junctions, and the feasible size of stations is related to the space available above streets.

The widespread adoption of elevated track may have originated, in part at least, from the 1968 Cabtrack studies initiated at Farnborough.[1] These were some of the earliest detailed studies of the feasibility of an autotaxi system. The original estimates for the costs of the three types of track were (1968 prices, for single-line autotaxi track):

Elevated	£153,000 per km
Ground level	£152,000 per km
Bored tunnel	£354,000 per km
Cut-and-cover tunnel	£460,000 per km

On the basis of these estimates there is little to be gained in cost terms by building track at ground level rather than above ground. Tunnels, more than twice as expensive as elevated track, fail to provide an attractive alternative. Our own cost estimates for the three types of track suggest a quite different relationship (see Table 4.1). Ground-level track appears to cost about 30 per cent as much as elevated track, compared to which tunnels prove only a little more expensive. The difference between the two sets of estimates is to some extent due to developments in construction techniques over the last six years. There is some evidence that tunnels are also beginning to compete with elevated roadways.[2]

Our estimates were gained by examining the costs of similar structures, such as footbridges, roadbeds and large sewerage tunnels. We also asked engineers with experience of this type of construction to estimate the extra cost that may arise from the special structural loads and requirements of a vehicle track. This method was adopted because it was felt to

Table 4.1

Cost of track construction in 1973

	Unit	25-passenger vehicle		4-passenger vehicle	
		Single track	Double track	Single track	Double track
Track width	m	3·0	6·0	2·0	4·0
Tunnel diameter	m	3·5	6·0	2·2	4·0
Elevated construction plus track heating	£/m	570	1,050	420	760
Ground-level construction, track heating, fencing, and land	£/m	160	310	130	240
Bored-tunnel construction	£/m	660	1,380	450	800
Cut-and-cover construction	£/m	700	1,550	430	1,010

Individual costs included in the above estimates are:

Heating of track		
3m wide (2m of heating)	£/m	14
2m wide (1·5m of heating)	£/m	10·5
Fencing (1·83m high)	£/m	2·5
Land	£/m²	9
Power supply for single track	£/m	37

be the most suitable means of including extra costs such as the movement of underground services, and diversions to traffic during construction. Estimates were based on 30 construction projects in British towns and refer to two representative sizes of bottom-supported vehicles. Their major dimensions are given in Table 4.2. Tunnelling costs refer to Coventry conditions, which are favourable, with little faulting, and to rocks similar to those found in the West Midlands. (See Table 4.3)

Table 4.2
Vehicle dimensions relevant to track design

Dimension	Unit	Autotram (25 passengers)	Autotaxi (four passengers)
Vehicle: height	m	2·6	1·8
width	m	2·0	1·5
length	m	4·5	3·0
Track-bed width	m	2·0	1·2
Wheel track	m	1·3	0·9
Vehicle mass	t	4	0·8
Passenger mass	t	2	0·4

Before going on to consider the three main choices in type of track, elevated, ground-level and underground, it is worth remembering that other alternatives are possible. Track could, like roads and railways, be placed on embankments, and where space permitted these would usually be cheaper than elevated track. It has also been suggested that, if track is placed in a shallow cutting, sewers and other services would not be disturbed, while the problem of severing rights of way could be avoided by providing frequent simple bridges over the track. This scheme might, for example, be employed in front of houses set back from the road, where an overhead track would be unacceptable but a sunken track with frequent crossing points feasible.

Elevated track

Track mounted on a viaduct permits routes to be built above streets without restricting traffic and pedestrian flow, but it does not give the freedom provided by bored tunnels, which can be planned with little reference to the building layout above them. The unsightliness of track overhead is one of its major drawbacks. This problem is considered in more detail in Chapter 9.

The basis of nearly all modern designs of overhead track is a series of uprights across which beams are placed to form a pathway. This trestle construction may be made from concrete, steel, or a combination of both. The horizontal beams may be 'simply supported' (each beam unconnected to its neighbour), or 'continuous', with all beams interlinked. The latter

Table 4.3

Main UK conurbations and their underlying geology

Conurbation	Population (millions)	Area (km²)	Approx. distance across area (km) Mean	Max.	Main geological strata to depths of approx. 50m	Geological structure	Major sub-aqueous work
Greater London	8·2	1,870	48	56	Brickearth, sand and gravel cover to west; Bagshot and Claygate sands; London clay; Blackheath and Woolwich sand; pebbles and clay; Thanet sand; chalk	Very little faulting	Thames
West Midlands	2·3	700	29	40	Almost half the area is covered with boulder clay; some sand and gravel; Keuper marl and sandstone; Bunter sandstone and pebbles; coal measures with few igneous intrusions	Considerable faulting	None
Merseyside	1·4	380	24	32	Very largely boulder-clay cover; little sand; Keuper sandstone; Bunter sandstone and pebbles	Some faulting	Mersey
South-East Lancashire	2·4	980	32	45	Cover almost completely boulder clay, sand and gravel; Bunter sandstone and pebbles; coal measures; millstone grit to north	Considerable faulting	Manchester Ship Canal and Docks
West Yorkshire	1·7	1,250	40	45	Coal measures; millstone grit; very little boulder clay	Heavily faulted	None
Tyneside	0·9	230	16	26	Cover almost completely boulder clay; coal measures with few igneous intrusions; magnesian limestone in extreme south-east	Considerable faulting	Tyne
Clydeside	1·8	880	19	39	Boulder-clay cover; coal measures with some igneous intrusions; millstone grit; carboniferous limestone; basalt	Heavily faulted	Clyde

Source: Transport and Road Research Laboratory Report LR 326.

method makes it possible to use lighter beams (or longer spans, about 30 per cent longer),[3] but these may suffer from stresses set up within the structure — for example, owing to a column settling. In an open space this type of structure could be built comparatively cheaply, but in a built-up area additional constraints would make the construction more expensive (by up to 25 per cent).

1   It will not always be possible to space the upright columns evenly, owing to roads and other obstructions. Columns may need to be spaced closer together on curves, in order to provide an efficient structure. When the track is situated over the centre of a road, it may be necessary to arrange support columns so that their bases are not directly under the track.

2   Horizontal and vertical curves and transitions into curves will be frequent on a track that is introduced into an existing town (Platts[3] suggests that in an urban area over 50 per cent of track may be curved).

3   It will not usually be possible to have full access to the site during construction, and this may increase the contractor's costs. He will probably be restricted to working at hours when streets are not in heavy use, and may have to use depots and storage areas at some distance from the place of construction.

4   There can be great variation in the costs incurred for foundations and moving services away from foundations. In a survey of footbridges, we found that foundation costs varied from £750 to £2,700 per column. The cost of moving services varied from £4 per m of bridge to £45 per m.

Loads on elevated track

The loads that bear on elevated track include self-loads due to the track itself, vehicle loads, and occasional loads.

Self loads. The main vertical loads on the foundations and columns are caused by the mass of the elevated structure. The vehicle mass is often a trivial addition. This feature is even more pronounced in the case of lateral overturning moments due to wind pressure. The side area of the track is usually greater than that of the vehicles, and the wind load on the track is often the most important factor in design.

Vehicle loads. The mass on the vehicle has only a small influence on foundation designs, but a much greater influence on the design of the elevated beam. Both the mass of the vehicle and its manner of support, concentrated loads or distributed, have a marked influence on beam design. Likewise, the position of guidance rails may significantly affect the beam design. The problems of beam shape are considered further in the next chapter. Vehicles also apply lateral and torsional forces on curves, according to their speed, braking forces along the track, and dynamic forces related to the quality of the track surface, the speed of the vehicle, and its type of suspension.

Occasional loads. During construction, elevated track and its components may experience loads greater than those to be encountered in service. A test track built by Tracked Hovercraft Ltd suffered from these loads. During erection, new beams were transported along previously erected ones, putting a greater load on the supporting beams than they would have to bear when in service; on one occasion a beam fractured and a section of track collapsed. Even when in service, there are many loads of this kind. Ground subsidence has already been mentioned. Accidents on the track may cause additional loads or a sudden concentration of vehicles. Track-borne rescue and maintenance vehicles may be heavier than passenger vehicles. If the track is built above street level, a road vehicle may collide with a column. In Britain, the Transport and Road Research Laboratory has decided that the track should, in this event, be able to resist the removal of one column without collapsing, although it might sag.[4] In Germany, Demag-MBB have produced columns that can resist being struck by a heavy lorry.

Elevated track design

At the moment, disagreement remains as to the relative merits of steel and concrete. Rolled-steel standard-section beams provide the cheapest means of constructing a trestle viaduct of the type described (see Fig. 4.1). Their major drawback is an unattractive profile, but steel track is often fabricated from sections and then clad with a more graceful non-structural cover. The resonance of such structures can be damped, although existing examples on railways are noisy. Rather than incur increased costs by providing a more attractive steel structure, a cast-reinforced concrete one may be substituted. Overhead footways present similar problems. Often, expensive concrete structures are adopted for both aesthetic reasons and the lower maintenance costs of concrete. Rigidity, rather than ultimate strength, provides the main design criterion for most lightweight track structures, owing to the importance of limiting dynamic deflections of beams as vehicles traverse them.

Approximate costs at 1973 prices of superstructure are, per m^2 of deck area:

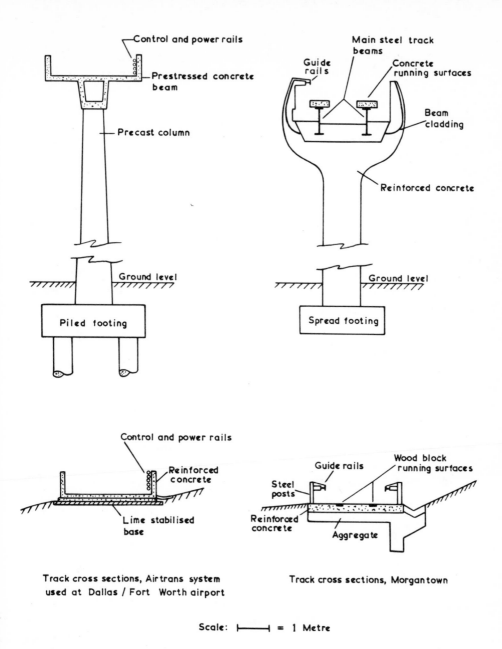

Track cross sections, Airtrans system
used at Dallas / Fort Worth airport

Track cross sections, Morgantown

Scale: ├────┤ = 1 Metre

Fig 4.1.   Track cross-sections. The elevated track used at Dallas/Fort
Worth is constructed entirely from concrete, whereas at Morgantown a
steel/concrete composite construction was used. The Morgantown track,
which carries smaller vehicles than those at Dallas/Fort Worth, is
particularly massive

£50–80 – steel construction from standard rolled-steel joists;
£70–90 – concrete, precast or *in situ,* reinforced or prestressed;
£130   – a spine box of welded steel.

Practically all designs are of the simply supported type.

There is also controversy over the most desirable column spacing for elevated track. Early work focused on attempts to minimise the total cost of foundations, columns and beams; for example, research at Carnegie-Mellon University[5] found 15m to be the optimum column spacing for most track. Since then, Platts[3] has argued that long spans are necessary so that road and other crossings can be made without the need for special spans; whereas Robert Matthew, Johnson-Marshall and Partners[4] consider that short spans suit the scale of streets better and are thus less oppressive. Foundations can be simple spread footings (a flat lump of concrete about 1m below the surface) or in poor ground may consist of a series of concrete piles down to firm ground.

Ground-level track

Ground-level track is the cheapest form to construct, in spite of three factors that reduce this advantage:

1   Some degree of access between the two sides of the track must be maintained. This may entail overbridges or underpasses that significantly raise the overall cost.
2   The land on which the track is built ceases to be available for other purposes and may need to be purchased. Approximate costs of land in Coventry in 1973 were: for good industrial land, £150,000 per ha; for poorer land of an awkward shape or with bad road access, but suitable for a reserved-track route, £90,000 per ha (this is equivalent to about £54,000 per km of double track for autotrams and £36,000 for autotaxis).
3   Although ground-level track is generally less obtrusive than elevated track, it needs to be protected with fencing. The fencing itself may be considered an eyesore in many surroundings.

Bottom-supported vehicles that operate in a trough-shaped track can generally run on a tarmacadam or concrete surface that could be constructed with current roadmaking equipment and techniques. The sides of a trough track or a central track spine could either be made from concrete as an integral part of the roadway, or fabricated from steel components fastened to posts (see Fig. 4.1). Both methods have been used on test tracks. Vehicles with other types of support, particularly suspended vehicles, gain little by operating at ground level. Economies derived from lower and simpler supports may be absorbed by the extra costs of land and fencing. Although British towns do not contain many wide streets suitable for overhead track, there are situations where old rail rights of way and central road reservations can be used for ground-level track. Even in Coventry it was found that over 60 per cent of track could be placed at ground level on the chosen routes (in a denser network, the proportion would fall).

The need for access across a ground-level track limits the extent to which roads and central reservations can be used. However, it seems likely that certain transverse paths could be severed without an overall loss. For example, if ground-level track on a central reservation passed one end of a residential street, it might be worth banning traffic from crossing the reservation to reach the street. Not only would this permit a route to be built at ground level, but it might also make the street quieter.

Track in tunnel

It has become common to build urban railways in tunnels, but automated systems are usually designed to be constructed overhead. The London deep-level tube railway is one of the few railways that was designed from the outset to make use of tunnels. The vehicles closely fit a tunnel bore of 3·85m diameter and differ in cross-section from the vehicles used on most automated systems; these are rectangular in section, with broad bases intended for elevated track.

Tunnels are of two main kinds: those bored from one or more points, and those that are first dug as a trench and then covered. The costs of the two methods are similar for tunnels of the size suitable for automated transport. Usually the cost of bored tunnels rises in proportion to the square of the diameter, since the cost is closely related to the volume of material to be removed. Cut-and-cover costs are often complicated by expense relating to the difficulty of using the site or moving services (see Fig. 4.2).

Bored tunnels can be built without reference to the street network and under obstacles such as rivers. Techniques of small-bore tunnelling are being developed rapidly, but the cost of bored tunnels can easily vary by a factor of 2, according to the rock conditions encountered. In particular, mixed hard and soft rock can be very troublesome, as the machines best suited to each are different.

Cut-and-cover tunnels must be built under roads or other land that can

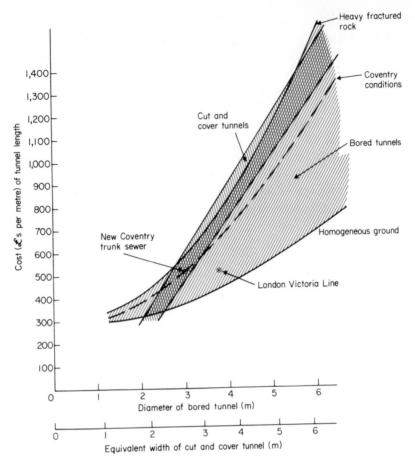

Fig. 4.2   Tunnel costs, 1973 prices

be made temporarily available for excavation. The tunnel must be near the surface, but it need not be of circular cross-section. Conventional earth-moving machinery can be used and there are fewer restrictions on space and access for the construction team. Nevertheless, the noise, mess and disruption experienced by people near the construction site usually means that it is an unpopular mode of construction with the public.

A track built in a tunnel does not need certain extras found on track above ground. Debris is not likely to fall on the track; trespass and vandalism will be less of a problem. However, lighting is needed, if only in emergencies. Drainage pumps and ventilation equipment are also needed, and it is necessary to make some provision for emergency escapes from the tunnel. Some advantages that stem from using tunnels, and could compensate for their high cost, are listed below.

30

1   Noise and visual intrusion are little problem, and hence noisy components such as steel wheels can be used.

2   Route lengths could be shortened if bored tunnels that do not need to follow the street network are used.

3   Wind loads would not affect vehicles.

4   A tunnel under a road need descend less than an equivalent overpass. In Britain, an overpass must have a clearance of 5·1m, whereas an underpass for autotrams need have a clearance of only about 3·0m.

Owing to the unsightliness of elevated track and the small difference in cost between elevated and underground track, the future development of automated transport may depend on how well systems can be adapted to make the best use of tunnels, and to what extent routes can be planned to make use of short lengths of tunnel in critical areas, with cheaper construction techniques used where room is available.

Stations

It is worth clarifying why urban railways and automated systems require large structures of considerable complexity, when buses and trams operate successfully from a post in the ground. The reasons are listed below.

1   The transport route itself presents a barrier to transverse movement by pedestrians. In order that people can approach the station from both sides of the route, a crossing must be provided, either under or over the track.

2   The track is frequently not at ground level, and stairs, ramps, escalators or lifts must be provided so that passengers can reach platform level.

3   When the track is not at ground level, it is usually essential to have a waiting area at the same level as the track and to provide sufficient space at the top and bottom of staircases, and so on, to reduce the chance of accidents.

4   It is often worthwhile to have fare-collection equipment in stations rather than on vehicles, because: (a) with large flows of people, the number of vehicles tends to be high and, therefore, the amount of on-board equipment large; (b) it is easier to find room for and supervise automatic ticket equipment in stations rather than on board automated vehicles.

Thus, the unavoidable expenses incurred in station construction are mainly related to the provision of passenger facilities and occur due to the segregated nature of the track. In this respect, automated transport stations differ little from stations on conventional urban railways. If the station is unmanned, there will be a particular need to ensure the safety of passengers, but this is not unique to automated systems. Conventional railways may also have unmanned stations. Owing to the short headways at which automated vehicles are likely to operate, the facilities for vehicles do need to differ. There are two broad types of layout to suit different average headways between vehicles. If the headway is long in comparison to the time taken to unload and load vehicles, then there is little need to clear the main track for other vehicles, and on-line stations are appropriate. As the headway becomes shorter, down to as little as one-thirtieth of the unloading/loading time, there is an increasing need to ensure that stationary vehicles do not impede moving vehicles, and 'off-line' stations become necessary.

On-line stations

An on-line station, suitable for vehicles operating with long headways, contains no branch tracks, and vehicles load and unload while stationary on the main line. The chief advantages of this type of station are simplicity and cheapness. As a penalty, the operation of vehicles is significantly influenced by the behaviour of passengers. Overall vehicle headway ceases to be controlled by the headway on open track, and is in part determined by the speed and number of alighting and boarding passengers. In most circumstances, a platform in the centre of a two-way track is the cheapest station layout, since additional facilities, such as stairs, can be shared by both platforms; but there are circumstances, such as where a station is placed on an existing route, when this may not be true. Simple stations of this form, with short platforms, are similar in operation to a normal metro station: automation makes little difference. However, owing to the small size of the platform, perhaps 10m long (see Fig. 4.3 for a comparison of station sizes), the major costs occur in the provision of escalators, stairways, booking offices, and similar facilities, rather than in constructing the parts of the station related to the vehicles. In the more complex types of station discussed below, the opposite tends to be true, and facilities for vehicles introduce the greatest expense. An on-line station might be able to cater for one vehicle every 20 seconds in each direction (180 an hour), but this would be strongly influenced by the length, and variation in length, of boarding times at each station. A service of this frequency would be easier to achieve if a regimented operating method were adopted, vehicles departing after a set period irrespective of whether passengers had finished boarding.

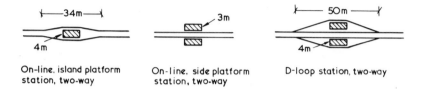

Full speed, off-line station, one-way

On-line, island platform
station, two-way

On-line, side platform
station, two-way

D-loop station, two-way

Fig. 4.3   Station layouts and their comparative lengths

Off-line stations

Off-line stations, suitable for vehicles operating at short headways, permit the maximum capacity of a track to be maintained without interference from vehicles stopping in stations. Whereas an on-line station limits route capacity, because vehicles in the station, and those slowing down and speeding up, impede others, vehicles destined for an off-line station can leave and join the main route at full speed. For this reason, off-line stations are used in situations where a continuous flow of small vehicles is needed.

The most common layout for off-line stations is: a branch from the main track that can be negotiated by vehicles travelling at full speed; a deceleration lane; a queueing space before the platforms; a set of boarding points, which may be in series or on parallel tracks; a queueing space in which to wait for a gap on the main line; an acceleration lane; and, finally, a lane that merges into the main track and can be negotiated at full speed (see Fig. 4.3). The overall length of such a station can be very large. For example, if the mean rates of acceleration and deceleration of the vehicle are $2\cdot5\,\text{m/s}^2$, the rate of change of acceleration permissible is $2\cdot5\,\text{m/s}^3$, and all manoeuvres are carried out separately (i.e. the vehicle does not decelerate longitudinally while on a curve), then typical overall station lengths would be:

33

Line speed (m/s)		5	10	15
Overall station length (m)		100	170	265

The overall width of the station is constrained by the width of track and platforms. If a station contains an island platform (i.e. one with platform loading/unloading facilities on both sides) and this is 4m wide and each track is 2m wide, the width of the station, including the main track, can not be less than 10m. There are very few urban streets in Britain that could accommodate overhead a station of this length and width. The length of the station can be varied by reducing the speed at which vehicles leave and rejoin the main track adjacent to the station, but this may also reduce the line capacity of the track (see Chapter 6). In addition, the amount of queueing space and number of berths can be reduced. The extreme case of this form of size reduction is a station with one berth reached by a branch line that can be negotiated only at slow speeds, perhaps 3m/s (see Fig. 4.3). This allows one vehicle to stop at the station while others go past; but the stopping vehicle must slow down on the main track and perhaps delay others in the process.

One variation of this type of station has two berths, one on the branch and one on the main line. Owing to its appearance, this form is often termed a 'D-loop' station. The two berths make it possible for this type of station to be used by about twice as many vehicles (i.e. about 360 an hour) as could use an on-line station, but it could not cater for the high frequency of vehicles that would use or pass most autotaxi stations (more than 1,000 an hour). In a given period, more autotrams could use a D-loop station, and passengers would, on average, need to wait a shorter time for a vehicle, than would be the case with an on-line station. However, the extra expense of the station, and the delay experienced by passengers while vehicles negotiated slow-speed curves at the station entrance, would probably cancel out the advantage.

Hump stations

If stations are placed on a hump, two advantages may be gained:

(1)   expensive stairs and escalators can be eliminated without serious inconvenience to the passenger (see Fig. 4.4);
(2)   as vehicles slow down when entering the station, their kinetic energy of motion can be translated into potential energy of height instead of being dissipated as heat in the brakes. This yields considerable energy savings.

34

Hump stations of this type will probably be worthwhile only when the track is underground and there is sufficient space available to have a surface level station.

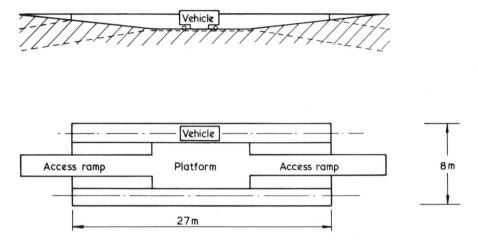

Fig. 4.4   A hump station layout for use with tunnel track

Station design and the passenger

The special demands made on station layouts by automated vehicles have been briefly considered above. Design for the passenger is similar in most respects to that on conventional metros, except that passenger flows will generally be smaller and the overall size of the station area available to travellers will therefore be less. This area may be subdivided into: platform areas where people wait for, board and alight from vehicles; service areas that contain facilities for issuing tickets, providing information, and staff accommodation (if stations are manned); and a queueing area at the entrance to the station, to cater for occasional peak demands.

Platform length is determined by vehicle or train length, whereas width varies little. Most London Transport stations are approximately 3m wide, regardless of passenger demand. 2m may be regarded as an absolute minimum for a platform serving vehicles travelling in one direction. Island platforms where a single platform serves trains travelling in opposite directions may economise on space: one 3m platform might be sufficient, but 4m would be preferable.

Where space is in great demand, there are advantages in placing the passenger service area on a different level from the platform and track

35

areas, and in using a single service area to serve passengers using vehicles travelling in both directions (this is common railway practice). It is also usually assumed that lifts or escalators are provided to link the passenger area and street level — on cost grounds, lifts are to be preferred to escalators. Owing to the desirability of having one service area, it is often necessary to place it on a third level, at neither ground nor track level. At track level there may be more than one platform and it may be undesirable to have a large structure, particularly above a street. If the

Table 4.4

Estimated station costs (1973 prices)

	Elevated		Ground level		Underground	
	Autotram	Autotaxi	Autotram	Autotaxi	Autotram	Autotaxi
On-line island platform station:	£20,600	£26,600	£30,600	£31,800	£24,800	£36,800
D-loop island platform station:	£82,600	£95,600	£59,600	£64,100	£97,600	£115,600
Off-line high-speed turn-off station:	£420,600	£347,600	£155,000	£139,500	£493,600	£373,600

Basic costs

PLATFORMS. Autotrams are assumed to operate from platforms of 10m x 4m; autotaxis or trains of autotaxi vehicles from platforms of 25m x 4m. Costs per m^2: elevated, £100; ground-level, £20; underground, £200.

BUILDINGS. Each station is assumed to have 20m^2 of building. Costs per m^2: elevated, £180; ground-level, £100; underground, £200.

STAIRS AND OVERBRIDGES. These vary in extent for each station; ground-level stations need most. Cost per m^2: £150

LIFTS AND ESCALATORS. Each station is assumed to have one lift to each platform. Costs: lifts (5m rise, 4—5 passengers), £10,000; escalator (5m rise), £20,000.

TRACK. The cost of track is included only when it is additional to the through lines.

LAND. This is only included for ground-level stations. Cost per m^2: £9.

TICKET EQUIPMENT. This is not included in the above estimates and could vary greatly. £15,000 might equip a simple station.

track is 5·1m above street level, in order to clear the traffic, there may be room for a mezzanine floor level; but lifts and escalators then need to be duplicated, increasing the cost of the station.

Costs

In many respects, stations are the least satisfactory part of automated transport systems. Either they are moderate in size and severely limit the performance of the network, or they are very large, very expensive, and make it difficult to design a system that can suit urban areas. Their design polarises to either the very simple on-line station or the full off-line, since D-loop stations and similar intermediate forms appear to offer no real advantages. On-line stations will probably be used with autotrams and off-line with autotaxis.

Table 4.4 shows some cost estimates of different station layouts. The costs are derived from standard architectural sources and equipment manufacturers, and also make use of the costs given in Table 4.1 for track. They demonstrate that most of the expense incurred in building a small station stems from passenger facilities such as escalators, booking offices, and so on; whereas, with a large off-line station, the additional track required accounts for a high proportion of the cost. A simple on-line ground-level station requires more escalators and lifts (if these are provided at all) than does an elevated or underground on-line station, and is therefore more expensive than one might expect.

Notes

[1] Urban Transport Technology Group, *Cabtrack Studies,* Royal Aircraft Establishment, Technical Report 68287, 1968.

[2] 'Tunnelled or elevated? Prices differ little', *The New Civil Engineer,* January 1974; C.D. Brown, 'Homes and highways', *The Consulting Engineer,* November 1974.

[3] M.J. Platts, 'Track design criteria in the development of urban transportation systems', in I.G. Black *et al., Advanced Transport Systems in British Cities. Symposium 74 Proceedings,* Warwick University, 1974.

[4] *Minitram in Sheffield,* Robert Matthew, Johnson-Marshall and Partners, 1974.

[5] *Urban Rapid Transit Concepts and Evaluation,* Carnegie-Mellon University, 1968.

5 Vehicles

Improvements in control technique have provided the main reason for increased interest in automated urban transport, but at the same time it has been suggested that developments in other aspects of vehicle design might be combined with automation to improve the overall design and performance of the vehicles. The most important of these developments are magnetic suspension, air suspension, and the use of linear motors for propulsion. Also of importance is the position of the vehicle relative to the track (suspended, bottom-supported) and the cross-sectional shape of the track. These factors have a considerable influence on the size and appearance of the track beam, the propulsive power required, the braking distance, the type of switch used, and the noise generated by the system.

Some of these suggested improvements could also make a great difference to the cost and performance of the system. For example, a suspended vehicle may easily be built to suit a small enclosed track, and can be designed to swing on curves in order that passengers do not experience lateral forces. This type of vehicle will have very different characteristics from one that runs in a trough-shaped track with high sidewalls. The latter, unlike the suspended vehicle, could be placed at ground level, and the trough might partially shelter the vehicle from side winds, though it would probably collect snow and rubbish. In addition, it may be more oppressive when mounted overhead in towns.

Ambitious and often exaggerated claims are still made for these different methods of supporting and propelling vehicles, but until recently very little work had been done to assess their relative merits. Although certain advantages of each may be known, the value of these characteristics has not been investigated in detail. For example, it is known that a disadvantage of a trough-shaped track is its tendency to collect rubbish, while a beam track that carries a straddle vehicle is awkward to switch. However, the relative nuisance of cleaning the rubbish from trough tracks and building complex switches for beam tracks has not been examined.

This lack of analysis has partly been encouraged by the tendency of manufacturers to develop and sell a complete system. A buyer usually has a choice between menu A and menu B and only rarely has the opportunity to select or value the different dishes. The manufacturer, free to decide the menu himself, has tended to concentrate on the form of suspension incorporated into the system (wheel, magnetic-levitation, or air-cushion) rather than on other aspects, even though the choice of the form of suspension does not have a very great influence on the performance of the system.

The main aspects of vehicle design are considered below, starting with the size of the vehicle cabin, which determines in part the proportions of the rest of the system. Then follows a discussion of the geometrical relationship between vehicle and track, and, finally, the technical alternatives for methods of suspension, guidance, propulsion and switching.

Vehicle proportions

Two demands on vehicle proportions conflict:

(1)   small vehicles are in general more visually acceptable in towns and, in addition, use cheaper track and lead to shorter waiting times;
(2)   for a given route capacity, carrying passengers in small vehicles is generally more expensive than carrying them in fewer large vehicles.

The size of vehicles determines the minimum size of tunnels and bridges and has a significant influence on the width of track. The greatest savings in the cost of track can be obtained by reducing vehicle cross-section rather than vehicle length. For small vehicles, the minimum cross-section is, to a large degree, governed by human proportions. The height of the vehicle is determined by whether passengers stand or sit. A minimum internal height of about 2m is needed for standing passengers and is generally exceeded on public service vehicles. Seated passengers tolerate very low roof heights in private cars, but a public vehicle for seated passengers would probably need a height of 1·5m. The dimensions preferred by passengers in private cars have been investigated in some detail, whereas much less work has been done to establish the needs of passengers on public transport. MIT[1] and RAE Farnborough[2] have made studies of the ideal dimensions for seated passengers. The work conducted at RAE Farnborough arrived at a seat module (i.e. seat plus area for feet) of 700mm wide and 1400mm long, whereas MIT give dimensions of 560mm wide and 870mm long (710mm to the knees). The MIT dimensions, which have been used in our work, appear to be nearer current public transport standards (seat widths vary from 480mm, for new metro vehicles in Paris, to 540mm, which is the new German standard for metros; seat pitch − i.e. the length of passenger modules − varies from

40

about 740mm to 880mm). Detailed dimensions of a seat module are shown in Fig. 5.1. The arrangement of modules is governed by a number of factors, of which the main ones are:

(1) the seats should be arranged as compactly as possible without dead areas of floor that cannot be reached for cleaning or use by standing passengers;
(2) passengers in all seats should be able to reach the doors easily, and there should be no points of congestion;
(3) passengers should be able to escape easily in an emergency, which may mean passing down a train of vehicles to an end exit;
(4) passengers should be secure at all times − for example, handholds should always be available;
(5) the arrangement of seats should not result in an unstable vehicle design (narrow vehicles less than two seats wide, and short vehicles with only one row of seats, can create this problem);
(6) certain layouts of vehicle support may necessitate seats in specific places, so that equipment or suspension can be accommodated underneath (a common example is found in the lateral-facing seats above the rear wheels of many buses);
(7) it may be advantageous if the seating arrangement can also accommodate prams and wheelchairs.

Some of the most common seating arrangements are illustrated in Fig. 5.2. A gangway width of 0·44m has been adopted, though considerable variation might be appropriate under some circumstances. The first four illustrations in Fig. 5.2 show the main transverse seating options. Vehicles one-seat wide are rarely given serious consideration, both because of their instability and because access to the seats needs a large number of doors for the number of passengers carried. Two-seat wide vehicles are popular for autotaxis, as they are stable, small in cross-section and, with four seats (see Fig. 5.2(e)), can accommodate most groups of travellers. However, Demag-MBB have adopted for their autotaxi a single forward-facing seat (1·5m wide) that can accommodate two passengers, or three in slight discomfort. A single row of lateral-facing seats has been adopted on some neverstop systems,[3] but has not found favour on automated vehicles. Autotram vehicles are usually rather wider than autotaxis and can therefore have more flexible seating arrangements. Both taxi and tram developers often make the width of the vehicle cabin similar to its height. However, the standard four-abreast seating with a gangway, common on buses and metros, is generally considered too wide. Lateral-facing bench seats on either side of the vehicle is a common arrangement (Fig. 5.2(i)).

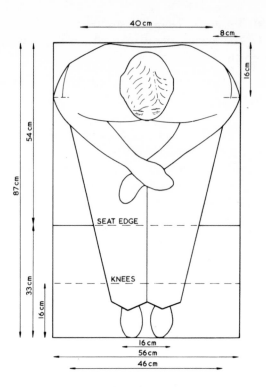

Fig. 5.1   Suggested standards for seat dimensions

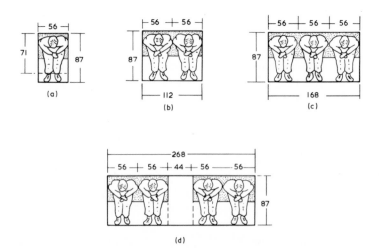

42

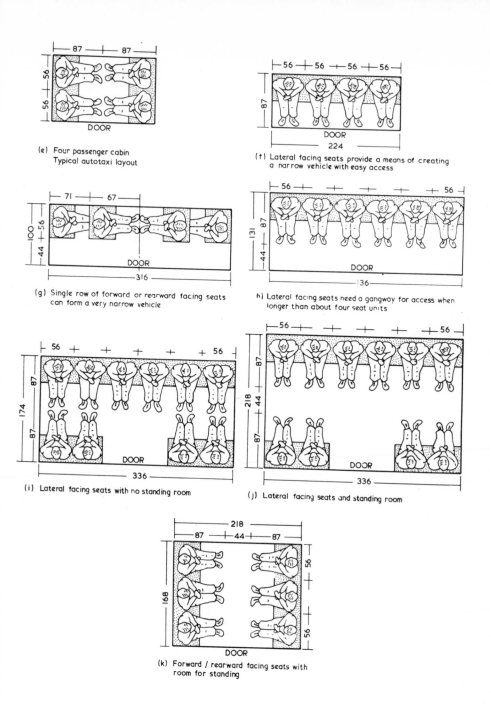

(e) Four passenger cabin
Typical autotaxi layout

(f) Lateral facing seats provide a means of creating
a narrow vehicle with easy access

(g) Single row of forward or rearward facing seats
can form a very narrow vehicle

h) Lateral facing seats need a gangway for access when
longer than about four seat units

(i) Lateral facing seats with no standing room

(j) Lateral facing seats and standing room

(k) Forward / rearward facing seats with
room for standing

Fig. 5.2   Alternative seating arrangements

For short vehicles, seats three- or four-abreast at the ends of the vehicle provide a convenient answer (Fig. 5.2(k)), particularly when doors are required on both sides of the vehicle. Seating layouts become more complex, and the available seating area rapidly diminishes, if access to the ends of the vehicle must be retained for emergency use and doors are required on both sides of the vehicle.

On London Transport,[4] standing passengers are considered to need about $0.30m^2$ each when the standing area is small, though this may be reduced to $0.14m^2$ when there is a large area available and crowding is only for short periods. In Paris, on the other hand, only $0.17m^2$ is considered necessary, and as little as $0.10m^2$ in crush conditions.[1] If the most generous London Transport allowance, $0.30m^2$ per person, is adopted, standing passengers can be accommodated at nearly twice the density of seated passengers. Although this is a notable increase, it necessitates higher vehicle cabins and may restrict the rates of acceleration to which the vehicle can be subjected.

In practice, autotaxi vehicles, between 1.3 and $1.5m$ wide and between 1.6 and $1.9m$ high, can usually pass through a tunnel 2 to $2.2m$ in diameter. Most designs for autotrams envisage a vehicle of between 2 and $2.2m$ wide and 2.6 and $3m$ high. There are occasional exceptions: the vehicle being developed by Krauss-Maffei, for example, has magnets underneath the track and is thus a particularly tall vehicle $(3.2m)$. Autotram vehicles can usually pass through a tunnel of 3 to $3.5m$ diameter (a London tube tunnel has a diameter of $3.85m$). It is possible to design autotram vehicles with smaller cross-section dimensions than those currently being developed. This may be particularly important if a high proportion of the transport route lies through a tunnel, though a tunnel diameter of below about $2.7m$ makes it difficult to provide for standing passengers. The proposed dimensions published by the Transport and Road Research Laboratory for the Minitram project in Sheffield are for a small vehicle with dimensions as follows: internal width, $1.7m$; external width, $1.9m$; internal height, $2.0m$; external height, $2.6m$; and length, $4.0m$.

The minimum length of vehicles is restricted by the need to give a satisfactory ride to passengers. A very short vehicle, of below about $2.5m$ in length, is likely to be subject to excessive pitch. The maximum length of vehicles is usually determined by clearance problems on curves, and rarely by structural limitations of the type met on railway vehicles. Normally, autotaxis need to accommodate only three or four seats, and vary from $2.3m$ to $3m$ in length. The length of autotrams varies much more, from $3.5m$ to about $13m$. This variation is partly due to the curvature that it is anticipated the vehicle will have to negotiate. The French VAL system, which employs vehicles 13·2m long, has minimum radii on curves of 40m, whereas the Morgantown system, which has vehicles 4·7m in length, has curves of 9m radius. However, the length of vehicle is also related to the desired frequency of service and the expected travel demand. If the off-peak service is to be of high frequency, but there is little demand, it may be worthwhile for the operator to use small, short vehicles. The capacity of the system can be increased by running vehicles in trains. This was not favoured during the early development of automatic systems, but recently, as the problems of operating vehicles at close headways have been more clearly understood, developers have adopted the use of trains of vehicles with more readiness.

Trains of vehicles have a high aspect ratio (i.e. the ratio of the vehicle length to its width). In general, high-aspect-ratio vehicles or trains permit the cost of the overall system to be reduced, since they can operate on narrower track. The track accounts for a major proportion of the total system capital cost, and the expense it incurs is directly related to its width. Very approximately, surface- and elevated-track costs increase in proportion to width, whereas tunnel costs increase in proportion to the square of width. As a penalty, however, high-aspect-ratio vehicles or trains entail long platforms, a larger number of vehicle doors, and usually more complex and expensive vehicles. There is also, as described earlier, a lower limit to the practical width of vehicles.

As the trackwork of a system usually costs much more than either the vehicles or the station platforms, there seems to be good reason for re-examining the case for very small cross-section autotram vehicles, particularly in the case of systems with a high proportion of tunnel track. The size of autotaxis could not easily be reduced further, but autotrams could either be designed to the minimum size in which standing is feasible or even be designed solely for seated passengers and be of similar cross-section to autotaxis.

Nothing has been said so far about the space necessary for equipment and running gear on board vehicles. Usually this is kept either completely below the floor level of the cabin or above its ceiling, with perhaps lighter equipment under seats. The depth required under floor level on wheeled vehicles is usually determined by the wheel diameter and suspension movement, and varies from about 0·5 to 0·9m. Air-cushion vehicles usually have lower floor levels than wheeled vehicles, whereas, at the moment, magnetically levitated vehicles need higher ones. Suspended vehicles with equipment above the cabin are usually more complex in layout, but do not have a much greater depth of equipment. In addition,

45

vehicles that are supported both at top and bottom, or are supported asymmetrically on one side, have from time to time been proposed. Although these proposals have some interesting attributes,[5] they have not been seriously adopted by a developer.

Vehicles and their relation to track shape

Long before the development of automated transport, inventors had been experimenting with different configurations of track and vehicle in attempts to improve upon the conventional railway. Their suggestions have included suspended vehicles, vehicles that straddle a beam, and trains with rubber tyres. Many of the same basic concepts have reappeared in the course of the development of automated transport.

In the case of track, some of the attributes that developers find desirable and seek to incorporate in new designs are:

(1)   a track shape that is structurally simple and cheap to manufacture;
(2)   a combined vehicle and track cross-section that is compact and will suit a small tunnel;
(3)   a track shape that is elegant and unobtrusive;
(4)   a track surface that does not trap debris;
(5)   a track shape that mechanically restrains a vehicle from overturning;
(6)   a track and vehicle combination that permits a simple and cheap switching arrangement to be constructed; and
(7)   a track surface that can also form an escape route when passengers abandon a vehicle (some authorities maintain that a surface that can be used by pedestrians may encourage accidents).

The choice of track shape cannot always be divorced from the method of vehicle support, but the main alternatives are discussed below.

Bottom-supported vehicles

Most developers favour using bottom-supported vehicles in which the centre of gravity of the vehicle is above the points of contact of the vehicle with the track. The different categories of bottom support can be distinguished by their means of lateral guidance.

1   Those that have the guidance equipment in the centre of the vehicle and inside the wheels or other device used for vertical support. The guidance is usually effected by means of a slot or spine in the track (see

46

Fig. 5.3(a)).

2   Those that have the guidance equipment outside the support devices. The guidance is usually obtained by sidewalls on the track (a trough track) or by the vehicle straddling the track and being guided by its outside faces (see Fig. 5.3(b)).

3   Those that have a single, longitudinal row of vertical support devices and have guidance devices that prevent overturning (see Fig. 5.3(c)).

4   Those that combine guidance and vertical support. This category includes: steel wheels that rely on their coning action to provide guidance; magnetic levitation, which involves magnetic forces that tend to centre the vehicle over steel rails; and various types of guidance signals that operate a steering mechanism on the vehicle and rely on wheel adhesion.

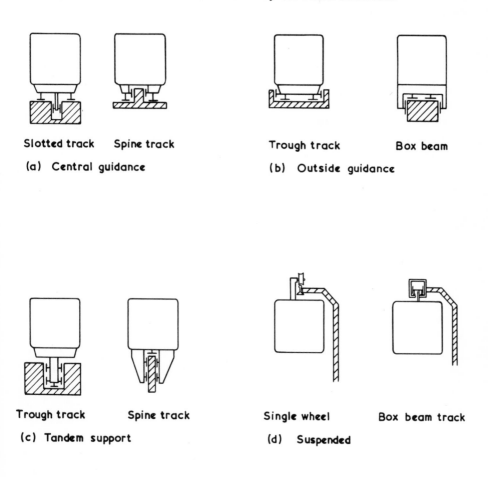

Slotted track   Spine track   Trough track   Box beam

(a) Central guidance   (b) Outside guidance

Trough track   Spine track   Single wheel   Box beam track

(c) Tandem support   (d)   Suspended

Fig. 5.3   Alternative track and vehicle cross-section

Central guidance

Central guidance by means of a slot in the track is used by all the major Japanese developers except the Kawasaki company. Central guidance by means of a spine along the track is used by the French Aérotrain company in its Tridim system (which also uses the central spine as a rack for rack and pinion propulsion) and by the German Demag-MBB consortium, which runs a separate set of vehicles underneath the track. In this case the track has a wide central spine, which forms the main structural beam, while support wheels run on shelves on either side.

If the central slot of a slotted track is left open in order not to trap rubbish, the side beams become separate structural members, and the design of a stiff structure, particularly in torsion, becomes more difficult. If the slot is closed underneath, rubbish, snow and leaves can be trapped. This may be a serious disadvantage when track is built at ground level. A track with a central slot provides a compact means of guiding vehicles. It has recently been adopted by Hawker Siddeley Dynamics Ltd, one of the two British firms developing autotram systems. However, in addition to the problems mentioned above, a central slot may provide insufficient space to mount current-collector rails, and switches are not easy to design, as the guidance spigot must pass through the support surfaces.

Although a track with a spine for guidance is less popular than a slotted track, it offers advantages: the spine can trap debris, but would be easier to clear than a slot; the track can more easily be made an efficient structural shape; and switches (which will be considered in more detail later in the chapter) can be of simple design, since only a section of the spine need be moved and there is a continuous surface for the support devices.

Outside guidance

Trough-shaped track is the most popular form of outside guidance being developed. In particular, most developers in the USA and France have adopted this form of track, whereas only two developers (Habegger Ltd and Toshiba Ltd) are using a box-beam track with vehicles that straddle the beam. In order that the track and vehicle should be compact, straddle vehicles are usually mechanically restrained from overturning. A box beam can be manufactured cheaply because it is an efficient structural shape both in bending and in torsion, but switches suitable for straddle vehicles are particularly difficult to design, as the guidewheels need to pass through the beam and the support wheels need to bridge the resulting gap. Both developers have resolved this problem by moving a complete section

48

of beam and replacing it with one of a different curvature — an expensive answer.

For structural strength, a trough track must normally rely on a box beam or I-section beams underneath the running surface, with some form of outrigger support for the trough sides or guide beams. Thus the trough shape (it is usually a shallow trough) is not as efficient a form as a box-beam track, though it is not much inferior. Switching is simple for vehicles in which the switching mechanism is on board the vehicle, since both routes can be chosen without breaks in the running surfaces. If the mechanism is on the track, however, it is usually necessary to move large sections of guidance beam in order to form the two routes (as on the VAL system, for instance). Three developers — Airtrans, Bendix and Uniflo — have succeeded in designing a switch that needs only a small moving element. This deflects the vehicle just sufficiently for its guidewheels to be trapped in an inverted channel on the trough side to which the route is set. Lastly, trough track tends to trap debris, and is often broader than the vehicles are. As the greatest breadth is near the base of the vehicle, this necessitates larger tunnel diameters than would be necessary with other track forms.

Tandem support

The Aerospace Company in the USA has developed a model of a vehicle that runs on a bicycle undercarriage in a trough and is guided by two tiers of guidewheels. The reverse of this, a bicycle undercarriage on a beam with guidewheels on either side of the beam, has not been used for urban transport, but was adopted for high-speed transport by Tracked Hovercraft Ltd. The Aerospace version of this layout necessitates a deep narrow trough, which is a poor structural shape for torsional loads, while the beam version would be as difficult to switch as other straddle vehicles.

Combined guidance and vertical support

Combined forms of support and guidance are associated with the characteristics of particular forms of suspension and will be considered in the next section. Steel wheels and magnetic levitation are being developed only in these combined forms, although both could employ separate means of guidance. However, rubber tyres can be used with separate guidance, or the two functions, guidance and support, can be combined in the same manner as on a conventional car. In this case, the lateral position of the vehicle can be constantly modified by the orientation of the front wheels relative to the back wheels, as long as sufficient adhesion is maintained between the tyres and pathway. All these methods usually necessitate some form of emergency restraint in case the normal means of guidance fail.

Suspended vehicles

Vehicles suspended below the track can be divided into those in which the vehicle can swing and those in which lateral movement of the vehicle is limited. Swinging vehicles neutralise lateral forces on the passenger while turning a corner (giving a similar effect to a bicycle) and do not impose torsional loads on the track (there may be other torsional loads on curves, owing to the weight of the track itself). Against these advantages, the vehicle may swing as a result of side winds and passengers moving around, and sufficient clearance from buildings and other vehicles must be provided. A light three- to four-seat vehicle might be particularly uncomfortable in high side winds, but larger vehicles – notably those used on the Wuppertal monorail in West Germany, and the Safege monorail – have been shown to be quite acceptable. The Wuppertal monorail has no lateral restraint and swings freely on curves, so that passengers do not experience a lateral acceleration while travelling around one. More recently, some degree of lateral stiffness has been incorporated into most designs. In particular, the suspended vehicle used by the Demag-MBB consortium cannot swing. Suspended vehicles can make use of practically all the basic forms of track shape that have been discussed for bottom-supported vehicles, but only two designs are in widespread use. The first, of which the Wuppertal monorail is an example, has a track that is a simple beam or rail. An arm on the vehicle hooks over this and is usually supported by a set of steel wheels. The second, and most common, track form is a box beam slit along its bottom face, so that an arm from the vehicle can connect with a bogie running inside the beam. The slit beam provides a protected running surface; but, if the vehicle is restrained from swinging, the track must be designed to resist torsional loads imparted by the vehicle. A slit beam is a poor shape for resisting torsional loads, and sufficient resistance to twisting can be provided only by increasing the bulk of the track. However, it seems that a compromise may be possible: the Rohr Monocab, for example, weighing nearly 2t fully loaded, restricts lateral swing of the vehicle to 5°, yet uses a modest track cross-section (760mm x 890mm).

All types of suspended vehicle need tall columns for mounting the track. On average, they need to be about 3m higher than those for a bottom-supported vehicle — 8m high rather than 5·1m where it is necessary to provide clearance over a roadway. A single track imposes an off-centre bending movement upon the supports, unless two supports are used to create a portal frame. Passengers must be provided with some form of escape ladder, since the track cannot be reached from the cabin in an emergency, and elevated station platforms need to be protected so that passengers cannot fall to the ground.

However, perhaps the biggest disadvantage of suspended vehicles arises where it would be possible to build track at ground level. As has already been shown in Chapter 4, ground-level track can cost as little as one-third of the equivalent elevated structure. The track for suspended vehicles is little cheaper to construct when built with the vehicles near the ground. Although the columns can be shorter, this saving is offset by the need to protect the track with fencing. A further drawback has been recently suggested in the report by Robert Matthew, Johnson-Marshall and Partners on the feasibility of constructing an elevated track in central Sheffield. Although their report is restricted to an examination of bottom-supported vehicles and track, they suggest that, in typical street surroundings, elevated track is least offensive when about 3m off the ground; when higher than that it becomes more oppressive. It would be extremely difficult to mount the track for suspended vehicles at a height of 3m (because it would not clear ground traffic), and thus, if this view is correct, suspended vehicles would be less easy to introduce into street surroundings than bottom-supported ones would. This is the opposite of the normal view.

Two tracks on one beam

The Demag-MBB consortium have developed for their Cabinentaxi system a track that makes maximum use of an overhead beam. The beam is a hollow box that is particularly deep (1·6m) and therefore stiff in both torsion and vertical deflection. Vehicles run both along the top of the beam and suspended underneath. The two tracks, top and bottom, are from a service viewpoint completely separate, and are used as two independent systems. However, the cost and intrusiveness of the track is probably not as much as would be incurred by separate tracks with separate beams. The system can also be constructed with only one track, or be constructed so that two beams and four tracks are supported by one column. This appears to be an elegant means of increasing the effective capacity of an autotaxi system, other than by decreasing vehicle headways as on a single track.

51

Vehicle weight

Developers have created an impression that recent designs of automated vehicles are particularly light, and that for this reason track and other components can be made more cheaply. However, most of the lightness of automated vehicles is due to their small size. When their mass per m² of floor area is compared with that of current public transport vehicles, the differences are not very great (see Table 5.1). It should also be remembered that existing rail vehicles are production models that are intended for a long life and heavy crush loads, whereas many designs of autotram are prototypes, built with expensive materials, that may need to

Table 5.1

Empty weight per unit floor area of public transport vehicles

	Vehicle-weight (t)	Floor area (m²)	Mass/area (kg/m²)
Tram[a]	20	51·1	391
Semi-metro[a]	42	97·8	429
Metro[a]	48	107·7	446
Economy light rail vehicle, Swiss Industrial Co.	16·5	36·6	450
Tatra K-2[b]	21·5	51·0	421
Single-decker bus	8·6	27·5	312
London Transport Victoria Line car	23	37·5	613
Skybus (Seattle)	11·4	30·3	376
VAL	11·5	27·0	425
Morgantown	3·9	9·6	406
Airtrans (Dallas/Fort Worth)	6·4	13·6	470
Transurban[c]	9·0	15·0	600
Uniflo[d]	1·0	5·9	169
H-bahn	2·5	8·1	309
Hovair[f]	3·3	11·5	287

[a] Design standards for public transport in West Germany.
[b] Six-axle, single articulated tramcar manufactured in Czechoslovakia.
[c] Magnetically levitated.
[d] Passive vehicle.
[e] Suspended vehicle.
[f] Air-cushion suspension.

be heavier when built in quantity. It is noticeable that most new automated-vehicle designs are in the range of 400 to 450kg per m² in weight. The exceptions usually have a novel form of support. The exceedingly heavy Krauss-Maffei vehicle relies on magnetic-levitation support, whereas the Otis air-cushion vehicle is light. Uniflo has produced the lightest vehicle of all, and this is almost certainly due to the incorporation into the track of all the support and propulsion equipment, though the fact that only seated passengers are permitted may also be significant.

There is little doubt that vehicles can be made lighter if it is felt to be worthwhile. Aircraft manufacturers go to great lengths to keep the weight of aircraft as low as possible. The higher the cost of an extra kilogramme on overall vehicle weight, the greater the costs worth suffering to save that kilogramme. Whether it is worth reducing weight by the use of expensive materials depends in part on the savings in fuel, and such-like, that result from the lighter weight. A comparison of the conditions under which existing public transport vehicles operate and those likely to apply to automated vehicles suggests that there may be some benefits to be gained by the use of lighter vehicles. One factor that clearly favours lighter vehicles is a high proportion of elevated track. In such circumstances, heavy components such as magnetic-levitation equipment become less easy to justify. Similarly, if high rates of acceleration are adopted, a lighter vehicle with a lower power requirement will be favoured.

Suspension and propulsion methods

The methods of suspension and propulsion for an automatic vehicle need be no different from the methods already familiar on railways. However, the operating conditions of an automated urban transport system are sufficiently different to have encouraged alternative solutions to the basic problems of supporting and moving a vehicle.

The conditions that are different from normal railway practice, and encourage (or do not discourage) change, are:

(1)   the envisaged reductions in scale of the track and vehicles, meaning that continuity with existing systems is not an important issue;
(2)   the importance attached to routes in streets and near buildings, necessitating quiet vehicles able to negotiate the tight curves and steep gradients found in urban streets;
(3)   close headways between vehicles and short distances between

stations, increasing the advantage obtained from high and accurate rates of acceleration and deceleration.

Both the steel wheel of a railway and a road vehicle's pneumatic tyre assist in the functions of supporting, guiding and propelling a vehicle, but in the development of automated systems there is a tendency to separate the equipment fulfilling these three functions. The system developed at Morgantown by Boeing uses pneumatic tyres to achieve all three, but several other systems use wheels for support and traction. Only magnetic levitation (being developed by Krauss-Maffei) combines guidance and support with a separate means of propulsion. It cannot yet be said whether systems that combine these three functions have any superiority over those where they are separate.

Methods of suspension

The principal methods being developed for supporting vehicles are:

(1)   steel wheels on steel rails;
(2)   rubber tyres;
(3)   magnetic levitation (by magnets attracted towards steel rails);
(4)   air-cushion suspension, the cushion being created by air jets generated on the vehicle or on the track.

Their power consumptions, either directly or as rolling resistance, are approximately as listed below.[6]

Steel wheels	15 kJ/t km
Rubber tyres	120 kJ/t km
Magnetic levitation	140 kJ/t km
Air cushion	140 kJ/t km

In comparison, the air resistance of a vehicle, which may vary considerably with different shapes and sizes of cabin, might absorb per square metre of frontal area 50 kJ/t km at 15/m/s, and the kinetic energy at 15m/s is 112·5 kJ/t. Typical vehicle designs embodying the four forms of suspension are shown in Fig. 5.4.

Wheels

A wheel permits motion along one axis and resists motion perpendicular to that axis — i.e. in the axis of the axle. This is usually beneficial for guided-vehicle applications where movement is desired along one axis only. If lateral movement, parallel to the axle, is desired in station areas,

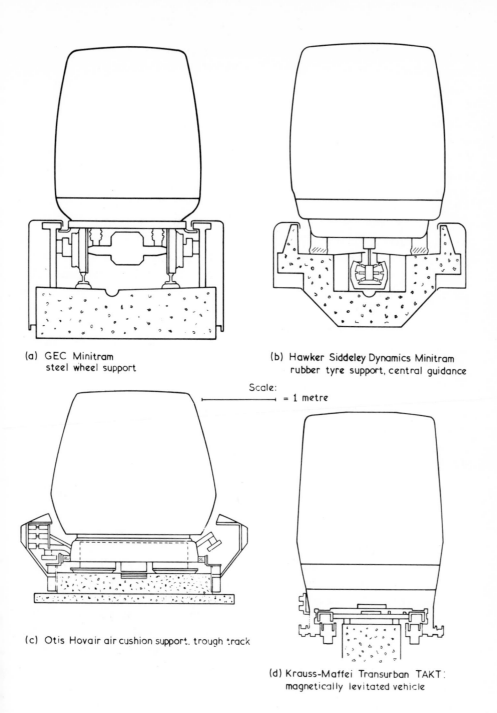

(a) GEC Minitram
    steel wheel support

(b) Hawker Siddeley Dynamics Minitram
    rubber tyre support, central guidance

Scale:
⊢————⊣ = 1 metre

(c) Otis Hovair air cushion support, trough track

(d) Krauss-Maffei Transurban TAKT:
    magnetically levitated vehicle

Fig. 5.4   Vehicle and track cross-sections proposed by developers

an extra mechanism of some form is needed. Unlike magnetically levitated and air-cushion vehicles, wheeled vehicles do not necessarily consume energy when stationary. Wheels do, however, present an unsprung mass that other forms of suspension can exclude, thereby making a comfortable ride easier to obtain.

Steel wheels. Steel wheels have been favoured for urban railways for many years, principally on account of their cheapness and reliability. They are cheap both in capital terms and in running costs. Several studies in the 1960s confirmed that they were still preferable for this purpose, though only three developers of automated transport (Aerial Transit Inc., Siemens AG and Easams Ltd) are planning to use them. Although conventional steel wheels were originally designed to be guided by the wheel flange, today it is generally accepted that some, or even all, the lateral guidance should be provided by the tapered shape of the wheel tread. The taper is arranged so that, when a vehicle wanders to one side, the outer wheel is running on a larger diameter than the inner. As they are on the same axle, the outer wheel travels forward faster and the vehicle is returned towards the centre of the track. The principal drawbacks of steel wheels are given below.

1 They are noisy. A recent study by Gramse[7] in the USA found that a test vehicle emitted $82dB(A)$ at 8m when travelling at 48km/h in a straight line, and $85dB(A)$ when on a curve of 9m and travelling at 8km/h. The American Department of Transportation recommends $57dB(A)$ at 8m — a noise requirement that is very severe compared with the present performance of public transport vehicles. It remains to be seen whether equally stiff requirements will be demanded in Europe, where many towns already operate urban steel-wheel vehicles. The problem of noise is discussed further in Chapter 8.

2 They can provide only limited adhesion. Steel wheels provide less adhesion than pneumatic tyres except under icy conditions. The co-efficient of friction employed for determining the starting load for rail locomotives in Britain is 0·24, and rail adhesion rarely falls below 0·2, even when there is oil on the track from diesel locomotives. Therefore, the adhesion required for the acceleration of 1·5 m/s^2 usually specified for vehicles with standing passengers can probably be obtained. The higher accelerations of about 2·5 m/s^2 used in most taxi systems could not be guaranteed, nor could the emergency rates of deceleration of up to 5 m/s^2 that have been planned by some autotaxi developers. Both acceleration and braking forces can, of course, be obtained independently of the steel

wheels, by means of magnetic brakes or friction track brakes, in which case they are comparable with air-cushion or magnetic-levitation suspension.

3   Steel wheels tend to be noisy on tight curves, but can, in the case of trams, negotiate curves of about 12m radius.

4   It is difficult to design a track switch for steel wheels that is actuated by a mechanism on the vehicle. Steel-wheel switches operated on the track are easy to build, are in widespread use, and are simpler than most of the alternatives developed recently. Switches that operate on board the vehicle have been designed,[8] but are less convenient than those for other methods of support.

The noise problem is probably the most serious deterrent to the widespread use of steel wheels for automated vehicles. If this can be overcome, they could be used much more widely, on account of their low cost and high reliability.

Rubber tyres on concrete or tarmacadam. Wheels with rubber tyres have been extensively developed for road vehicles, and several developers of automated vehicles have adopted very similar techniques using largely the same components (the LTV Airtrans vehicle and the Matra VAL vehicle are examples). Others rely on rubber-tyred wheels, but have made major adaptations in their use (as with the Demag-MBB Cabinentaxi, and Aerospace vehicles).

Rubber tyres have more resistance to motion than steel wheels have, and thus they have not been favoured for high-speed railways or heavy goods haulage by rail; but in urban transit other factors besides traction economy become significant. Tyres are probably superior to steel wheels in conditions where tight turns, steep gradients and frequent switching are encountered. They do, however, incur penalties: their rolling resistance is about eight times as large as that of steel wheels; at least one set of wheels must usually be steered or allowed to castor on curves; and guidance and switching equipment tends to be larger than for steel-wheel vehicles.

A conflict occurs between the rolling resistance of a tyre and its adhesion and quietness. A tyre made from high hysteresis rubber and with good adhesion makes more noise than a hard rubber tyre with poor adhesion. At one extreme is the policy pursued by Demag-MBB of using tyres solely for support and guidance. These tyres are solid and run on a smooth steel surface. The coefficient of adhesion, the rolling resistance and noise are all small, while traction, braking, guidance and switching all have to be supplied by other means. At the other extreme, the Boeing vehicles for Morgantown use their rubber-tyred wheels for support, traction, braking, guidance and switching. The tyres need to be able to supply sufficient adhesion for the fore-and-aft accelerations incurred in traction and braking and the lateral accelerations experienced in guidance and switching. As these characteristics must be maintained in all weathers, the tyres need to have a tread pattern, as well as be of reasonable diameter, pneumatic, and constructed of high hysteresis rubber. To complement this, the track must be constructed of a material (such as concrete or tarmacadam) that can give good adhesion. In order to retain adhesion in all weathers, the track surface may need to be heated.

Between these extremes there is a wide spectrum of designs: some types employ linear motors for traction and braking; some use arms giving lateral guidance, and switching that operates independently of the wheels; and some bias the steering, but rely on an alternative means of guidance for switching.

The general tendency has been to use separate equipment for each function on systems with sophisticated control requirements, and to combine the functions where the headways and routes are less demanding, as is the case for most autotrams. This is reasonable, since methods that combine these functions tend to compromise performance in one or more areas. Several systems provide an excellent ride and have such low tyre noise levels that other noise sources (such as current collectors) are the only ones noticeable.

Tyre wear and punctures are not likely to be a serious problem. The Paris Métro, which has been operating rubber-tyred trains for 18 years, has found that tyres last for over 300,000km and that punctures occur at intervals of about 20 million km.

Magnetic levitation

Interest in magnetic levitation has developed very recently and has centred on methods that use electromagnets attracted to steel rails. Other magnetic and electromagnetic methods have been considered, but are mainly applicable only to high-speed trains. In addition, methods combining magnetic levitation with propulsion are being developed, but these are still at an early stage.

The German firm of Krauss-Maffei has done the most work in developing devices for low-speed use (see Fig. A.1). Its vehicles are attracted up to steel rails on the track. It is necessary continuously to control the supply voltage to the magnets, as they are unstable in the vertical axis (the attractive force increases, the closer the magnets are to

58

the steel rails). The magnets, and hence the vehicle, are, however, stable laterally and no extra guidance system is required. Placing the magnets below the rails attached to the track does not prejudice whether the passenger compartment is above or below the track, but in the Krauss-Maffei system the passenger compartment is above, and, in the event of power failure, the vehicle drops onto skids on the track.

Thus, magnetic levitation of the form described relies on an active suspension to retain a gap between the vehicles and track (about 20mm between magnet and rail) and give a smooth ride to passengers. The suspension depends on an electronic system, which must measure the gap between vehicle and track (and also, perhaps, the velocity and acceleration between the two), then translate this into a stabilising fluctuation in the magnetic attractive force. This is the most complex form of suspension being developed, and its complexity is at present reflected in terms of cost and weight. It remains to be seen whether the cost, weight, performance and reliability of the system can be developed to match that of existing suspension methods.

The power requirement for magnetic levitation has not been definitely established. The DC power to levitate a vehicle without disturbing forces can be relatively easily calculated and is about 1kw per tonne. Trials or complex simulation are required to assess the power required when there are also perturbations in two axes (vertical and horizontal). The AC component needed to cope with these force variations necessitates higher peak voltages (about 10 times higher), which in turn need heavier insulation. The power needed to run the support system is probably 20 per cent larger than that needed to overcome the rolling resistance of a vehicle with rubber tyres. Maintenance will not involve the replacement of such things as tyres, air-cushion skirts, or rails — standard equipment on other systems — but it remains to be seen whether the replacement of failed electrical components amounts to a significant cost. Switching by magnetic means will probably always involve a second set of magnets, which increases the vehicle weight (the Krauss-Maffei vehicle weighs 9,000kg for a floor area of 15m^2). Non-magnetic methods of switching would, however, be practicable.

Magnetic levitation is quieter than wheel or air-cushion support,[9] but other noise sources, such as the noise of the current collectors, may be most significant. The electronic control of the suspension would probably give a comfortable ride, but equal expense on other support systems would provide results of similar quality.

Air cushions

Air-cushion vehicles have become accepted over the last fifteen years for marine use, and there have been many experiments with guided air-cushion vehicles. Three automated vehicle systems are under development. Two, those made by Otis (see Fig. A.5) and Aérotrain, feed their air cushions from fans on board the vehicle; the third (Uniflo) feeds its air cushion from fans inside the track. Air-cushion vehicles are the only ones of those discussed that can move sideways with the same ease with which they move forward. For this reason, lateral docking is used by two of the developers, Otis and Uniflo.

For support, air cushions probably need much the same power output per tonne of vehicle as magnetic levitation does. The final answer to this is unclear, because, although small airgaps need only a small power input, skirt wear tends to be heavy unless the track is smooth and clear of debris.

Air cushions for small low-speed vehicles produce little noise, although more than levitation magnets do. They need a broad flat track, which provides their most distinctive feature (the breadth of the track can often be greatly reduced for a suspended vehicle that does not require a broad base of support). Since the track supports a distributed load, it needs different structural design from, say, that for the concentrated loads produced by wheels. A system relying on air cushions could use a slightly cheaper track at ground level or underground, but elevated structures can be constructed more cheaply if loads are concentrated.

Some conclusions about suspension methods

The best form of suspension must meet three requirements: low cost, both in direct money terms and in power consumption and repairs; sufficient performance in terms of turning circle, adhesion (if required), ride quality, and so on; and small disturbance to non-users in terms of noise, size of track needed, and the like.

Cost

The two new methods, air-cushion and magnetic-levitation, are probably costly in all senses. They need most power and, owing to their complexity, are likely to be initially expensive. At present, however, air-cushion vehicles can be designed to be much lighter than magnetic-levitation vehicles. Steel wheels are the simplest method, since steering and guidance gear are not needed. However, although rubber-tyred wheels may necessitate more components, many of these could be standard items already manufactured for road vehicles, and the final cost may be little more than that for steel wheels.

Performance

Wheeled systems can provide sufficient adhesion in all but the most extreme circumstances of traction and braking, and can permit a cheap form of propulsion. In this they have an advantage over levitating magnets and air cushions, which do not have the option of combining the means of suspension and propulsion. Rubber tyres can provide more adhesion than steel wheels. Air cushions, the most manoeuvrable form of suspension, can easily negotiate tight curves and even translate sideways, but they are the only form of support that must be accompanied by a separate means of guidance. Steel wheels are manoeuvrable, but are noisy in the process; and magnetic levitation has proved awkward to design in a manner suitable for tight vertical and horizontal curves. It is possible to obtain an excellent ride performance with any of the four forms of support, if desired, as none of them restrict the form of suspension used. For example, mechanical springs could be incorporated on a magnetic-levitation vehicle, and active-height sensing suspension could be used in conjunction with steel wheels.

Disturbance

Of all forms of support, steel wheels are likely to be the most disturbing, owing to the greater noise they produce. Air cushions need a wide running surface, which might be obtrusive, but this is little worse than the conventional trough-shaped track favoured by many developers for rubber-tyred vehicles.

Thus, despite the fact that steel wheels are the cheapest form of support, the noise they make will prevent their being acceptable in all situations. Air cushions and magnetic levitation, which overall are more expensive than rubber tyres, have no significant compensating advantages and the possibility of greater unreliability, through being dependent on a power source for support.

Propulsion

On-board generation of power from fossil fuels is a well-tried method of supplying propulsive energy, but it is not normally considered acceptable for new forms of urban guided transport owing to the noise and pollution that is also produced. Nor is it necessarily the cheapest method available, particularly when there is a reserved track with the ability to provide a continuous source of power. Electrical methods of transmitting propulsive energy are today the most favoured for use on guided transport in towns. Mechanical methods (such as cableways and helical screws) are still under consideration, but are usually applied only to neverstop railways. The only automated system actively being developed that does not rely on electrical propulsion is Uniflo's. Air from the track reacts against vanes underneath the vehicle to impart forward motion. Although this method is less efficient than electrical means (per tonne), it permits a lightweight vehicle with no power-collection gear or motors to be used. This may provide an economic solution for transport corridors that have very high flow densities, but in most urban situations the high cost of the track will make the scheme too expensive. One other developer, LTV, has also considered a system with the major propulsion component off-board. [10] This scheme uses a linear induction motor drive with the motor stator coils in the track, the advantages and disadvantages of this being similar to those mentioned above. For the most part, rotary electric or linear electric motors on board the vehicle are found to be the most promising form of propulsion.

Propulsion by means of rotary electric motors and wheel adhesion

If wheels are employed to convert the torque of an electric motor into thrust, a range of types of rotary motor can be used. However, the propulsion is dependent on adhesion being maintained — either by the weight of the vehicle or by means of two wheels clutching a rail (the Fell system). One firm, Aérotrain, uses a rack and pinion drive to give both adhesion and guidance to an air-cushion vehicle.

Rotary motors are at present lighter and cheaper than the existing linear equivalents. They will probably always be lighter, because they can be geared such that the relative speed between rotor and stator is faster than that of the vehicle (for a given output, the mass of an electric motor is approximately inversely proportional to the surface speed of the rotor and stator), and the gap between the two moving components can be kept much smaller than is possible on a linear motor, in which one component is on the track and the other on the vehicle. Rotary motors are cheaper principally because they have been manufactured in large quantities for many years. However, it is necessary to have a gearbox in conjunction with a rotary motor, and, in the case of a rubber-tyred vehicle, either a differential or an independent motor for each wheel. It may one day be possible for linear motors, together with their reaction rail, to be manufactured more cheaply than a rotary motor and its attendant gear drives. Four main types of rotary motor are feasible for traction:

synchronous motors, reluctance motors, DC motors, and induction motors. The latter two are the most probable choices for automated urban transport.

DC motors

The DC motor is much the most common form of traction motor used today, both for conventional railways and for automated transport development. Current must be fed both to field coils that are stationary and to an armature that rotates. The current is usually fed to the armature through carbon brushes and a commutator, the performance of which limits the speed of the motor. Motors with series connection of the field and armature winding, or a part series, part parallel connection, provide the most satisfactory characteristics for traction purposes (see Fig. 5.5). Until recently, DC traction motors were voltage-controlled by adjusting the size of resistances in series with the motor. Today it is possible to feed

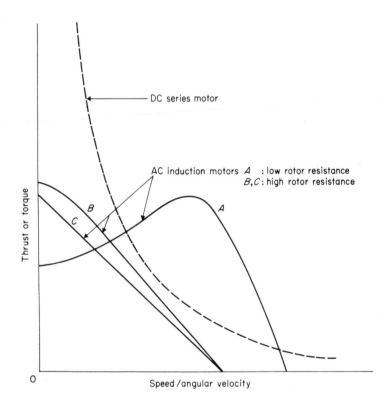

Fig. 5.5   Performance of AC and DC electric motors

to the motor a pulsed voltage that reduces the effective power without the losses inherent in resistances. This is usually termed 'chopper' control.

Induction motors

Induction motors are less frequently used for traction purposes, mainly because they cannot be controlled as conveniently as DC machines. However, they do not need either a commutator or a rotating set of coils, and can thus run at higher speeds and be made more compact. Control by voltage is possible, but the motor is then running at low efficiency and can overheat.

Three main methods can be used to overcome this deficiency:

(1)   feeding variable-frequency current to the motor through a variable-frequency invertor;

(2)   using a fixed-frequency invertor in the rotor circuit of a motor to vary the rotor resistance (slip-ring motor) and thus control the motor speed (this method was particularly favoured by RAE Farnborough); [11]

(3)   using a constant-speed induction motor to drive a variable-speed hydrostatic drive. This arrangement may also be used to replace axle differentials, since individual hydraulic motors could be placed in each wheel.

These methods are complex and largely untried, but may eventually replace the DC rotary motor.

Linear machines

As it is less than ten years since the serious development of linear electric motors began, their final potential is not yet known. Although most forms of rotary motor can be built in linear form, only the linear induction motor has attracted widespread interest. The Aerospace Company has proposed that DC linear stepper motors be used, and the Siemens Company is at an early stage in developing a suspended system propelled by linear synchronous motors. This discussion concentrates on the linear induction motor, but many of its advantages and disadvantages are common to the other types of linear motor.

Unlike a rotary motor, the relative speed of the two parts of a linear motor is determined by the speed of the vehicle. The most efficient relative speeds are over 200km/h for normal 50hz AC electrical frequencies. Most urban vehicles travel well below these speeds and therefore incur a weight and cost penalty. In addition, all types of linear motor suffer from end losses, which do not occur with rotary machines. As the two main components of the motor are split between the vehicles and the track and need to remain in close proximity for efficient operation, the suspension of the vehicle needs to cater for opposing demands: a motor that must follow the track with some precision, and a passenger cabin that must be given a smooth ride. In some instances, this has meant that the motor and cabin must be provided with separate suspensions. Nevertheless, the gap between rotor and stator on linear motors is usually about 20mm, compared with about 2mm for rotary motors. These problems also apply to a system that has the main motor windings on the track.

Most early development of linear motors was concerned with double-sided machines in which two stators on the vehicle sandwiched a reaction rail on the track. This provides an efficient layout, but more recently interest has also been shown in single-sided motors, which, although less efficient, can use a flush reaction rail on the track and only one set of coils. At the moment, both concepts are being developed for automated transport. The double-sided motor has the disadvantage of a fragile spine reaction rail, which may also make switch design difficult, whereas a single-sided motor suffers from unbalanced vertical forces between the reaction rail and the vehicle coils, making suspension design difficult. The problem of controlling a rotary induction motor has already been mentioned. The problem is the same, but more serious, when the motor is linear. Hydraulic drives are, of course, not possible; nor are slip-ring motors. However, whereas voltage control can cause a rotary motor to overheat rapidly, a linear motor can dissipate heat over a considerable length of track. This is the form of control most commonly used on linear-motor powered vehicles, despite other disadvantages such as poor power factor when starting and variable vertical forces. In the future, frequency variation by means of an invertor may be used to provide a more efficient motor, but at the moment such invertors are both heavy and costly.

It seems at present that wheel support is preferable to air cushions or magnetic levitation. Once wheel support is chosen, there seems to be no overall advantage in using linear motors rather than rotary motors and wheel adhesion for autotrams. The most likely use for linear motors is in autotaxi systems where high rates of acceleration are desired. However, most developers of these are at the moment developing wheel-supported systems with rotary motors.

Switching

There are two basic types of switch: those in which the movement of a mechanism on board the vehicle determines the route that the vehicle takes through a diverge, and those in which the movement of a mechanism in the track sets up alternative routes for the vehicle. If vehicles are travelling behind each other at very close headways, it is convenient to have the switch mechanism on board vehicles, so that they can be in the correct position for the chosen route at more than a headway distance before the switch. If vehicles travel at long headways, greater than the distance between switches, it is worthwhile having a mechanism on the track, so that it can be set to the correct route before the vehicle reaches the previous switch. Barnard and Rossignol [12] also point out that on-board switching requires a much more complex information linkage between the vehicle, the possible routes, and the control than is needed for off-board switching arrangements.

On-board switching

The most common form of on-board switch uses a mechanism that can drop a guidewheel down to run on the outer side of a trough-track wall. A wheel can be dropped on either side of the vehicle, and thus it can be made to follow either wall at a switch. The same principle can be used with other track shapes. The Boeing vehicles used at Morgantown have an ackerman steering system (road-vehicle steering), which can be biased to steer left or right (see Fig. A.3). A sensing wheel that can detect the side walls of the track then centres the steering when the vehicle is near the wall. The vehicle can be made to follow either wall of the track, and thus either route at a diverge, according to which way the steering is biased. This concept need not use a wall for a position signal: it could be adapted to use other position-signal sources, such as a buried wire. The Krauss-Maffei magnetically levitated vehicle uses a second set of magnets, which, as mentioned earlier, are operated in a given sequence to determine which route is taken at a diverge. The sequential operation is necessary to cross the gaps that must be left in the steel track at switches. The Siemens Company claims that its vehicles choose a route according to which of their two adjacent synchronous linear motors is in use. However, the mechanical methods of on-board switching are simple, and it seems that there is little to be gained by using electromagnetic methods involving a large amount of extra equipment. On-board switching seems warranted only on autotaxi systems with close-headway operation, and there is little prospect of widespread use of it with autotrams.

Off-board switching

The form and mode of operation of railway switches or points is well known and has remained unchanged for many years. They provide a base with which the newer methods may be compared. Two broad types of off-board switch can be identified:

(1)   those in which the vehicle continues to use its normal guidewheels while travelling through the switch;
(2)   those in which the vehicle temporarily changes to a separate set of guidewheels and guide surfaces, or uses additional wheels in conjunction with some of its normal guidewheels. In one or two cases vehicles have been designed that transfer to a different set of support wheels as well.

Systems that use only one set of guidewheels. These switches are usually characterised by a large element, which must move to set the switch. The element must be able to reproduce two separate paths with the same cross-sectional shape as the rest of the track. In the case of a trough track, this entails the use of an element large enough to block off the whole width of the trough at an angle (see Fig. A.4). The virtue of a conventional railway switch is that, owing to the small contact areas of the steel wheels, this type of switch can be made with small moving elements. The large size of the elements used in most recent designs of this type is reflected in the large amount of time required to change the switch from one route to another. The VAL, Rohr Monorail, Toshiba Mini-Monorail, and Mitsui Vona systems all use this type of switch, and need about 10 seconds to change the route setting. All these systems use one large element that either pivots about a vertical axis or slides laterally. However, the Habegger Minirail uses an element that pivots about a horizontal axis along the track, and, although the element would have a low moment of inertia about the axis, the switch can need up to 20 seconds to move. The KCV Company uses two smaller elements, which rise out of the surface of a trough track to form the walls for the two paths. This method needs smaller elements in conjunction with a more complex mechanism, but provides a faster action, needing only 3 seconds.

Systems that use a separate set of guidewheels. If a separate set of guidewheels and guide surfaces are used to determine the route taken by vehicles at diverges, the size of the moving elements and the distance they move is determined by the size of the guidewheels, rather than by the width of track necessary for vertical support. The three most advanced developers of this form of switch — LTV Airtrans, Bendix Dashaveyor, and Uniflo — have all applied it to trough-shaped tracks; not unnaturally, since trough track otherwise requires particularly large moving elements.

67

They all use a rail or channel at the side of the trough to trap a single wheel or pair of wheels on the vehicle. By moving the sections of channel at the point where the track begins to diverge, vehicles can be guided onto either route (LTV Airtrans and Uniflo have so designed their switches that only a channel on one side of the track need move). The developers all claim low switching times: 3 seconds for LTV Airtrans; 1 second for Bendix Dasheveyor; and 0·1 second for Uniflo. These switches appear to be superior to the conventional type requiring large moving elements. The switch itself can be very much cheaper, and the time taken to move the switch can be less. The necessity for extra guidewheels on the vehicles is a small penalty. However, the transfer between different sets of guidewheels may be difficult to achieve smoothly.

Reliability

A desirable attribute of any transport system is reliability — that is, infrequent interruption to the service by the breakdown or failure of one of the system's components. Alternatively, we can say that it is desirable to have the service available for as high a proportion of time as possible. In systems engineering, availability is normally defined as

$$A = \frac{MTBF}{MTBF + MTRS}$$

where
$\qquad A$ = availability,
$\qquad MTBF$ = mean time between failure,
$\qquad MTRS$ = mean time to restore service.

For instance, if $MTBF$ is 9·5 hours and $MTRS$ is 30 minutes, then A = 0·95.

Failure may be due to weather or, more usually, be confined to equipment failure. The desirability of a high A makes designers seek a high $MTBF$ and a low $MTRS$. Long periods between failures can be achieved by the use of redundant and duplicated components, regular replacement of equipment, a high standard of maintenance, or a combination of all three. Restoring the system to its normal state can be achieved quickly in various ways. It may be possible to isolate certain component failures and minimise the time for which the whole system is out of use. For instance, failed vehicles may be shunted into a siding by a following vehicle or towed off the track by specially designed recovery vehicles. It may be necessary to keep large amounts of equipment and a large number of maintenance personnel on standby to ensure that repairs are carried out quickly. The cost of these may reduce to a significant extent the advantages to be gained from automation.

The decision on what levels of *MTBF, MTRS* and, implicitly, *A* are desirable depends in part on the trade-off between the extra cost of maintenance and capital expenditure and the inconvenience caused to passengers by occasional breakdowns in the system. There are obviously many possible combinations of the variables involved in design and maintenance policies, and it will take a number of years before we can start to identify where in the space of opportunities the optimum policy might lie. At the moment, few figures on reliability are provided by manufacturers, though there is an exception in the case of the Morgantown system, which claims the following performance details.

MTBF: system 26 hours
station 78 hours
vehicle 54 hours
MTRS: 60 minutes (maximum)

The vehicles of the Airtrans system are reported to have a much higher *MTBF* (500 hours) and a *MTRS* of 30 minutes; no figures are given for other components. However, it would be unwise to place too much confidence in these figures until experience has been gained of extensive operation.

The vehicle in motion

Vehicles that operate any form of urban transport are continuously passing through a cycle — accelerating from rest to a cruise speed, cruising or coasting, and then decelerating back to rest. All automated systems follow this pattern. Although autotaxis may stop at stations less frequently than autotrams, they need to make rapid changes in speed in order to retain correct headways at junctions and to pass through curves at the correct speed. Autotrams generally operate between stations less than 1km apart (see Chapter 7), while London Transport plan new Underground stations at 1·5km spacings. For this reason, the maximum rates of longitudinal acceleration and deceleration of automated vehicles are usually regarded as more important than their maximum speed. Cruise speeds of between 40 and 60km/h (11−16·7 m/s) are probable, but will vary between installations (see Figs. 5.6, 5.7). Just as longitudinal acceleration is of increased importance on automated systems, lateral

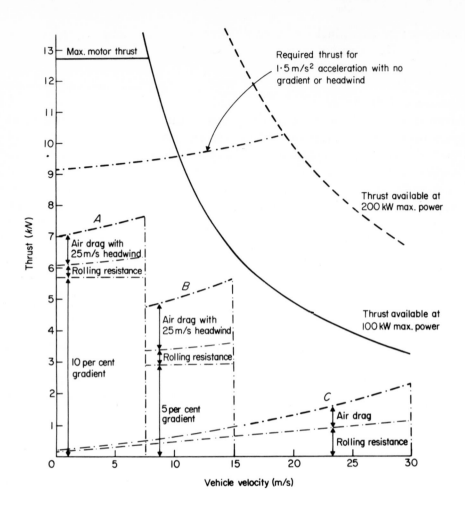

Key:
A   The total thrust necessary to sustain a steady speed against a 25m/s headwind and
     a 10 per cent gradient (shown up to a speed of 7·5m/s)
B   The total thrust necessary to sustain a steady speed against a 25m/s headwind and
     a 5 per cent gradient (shown up to a speed of 15m/s)
C   The total thrust necessary to sustain a steady speed with no wind or gradient

Fig. 5.6   Typical thrust and drag curves for a 6 t vehicle.

70

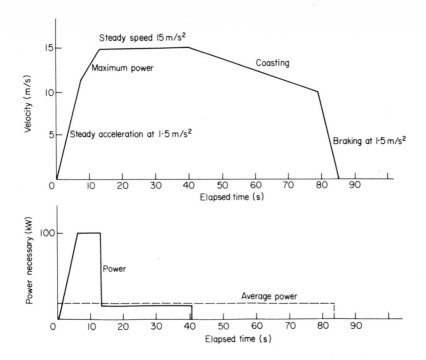

Fig. 5.7 Typical velocity and power curves for a 6t vehicle travelling between stations 1km apart with no gradient or headwind.

accelerations tend to be of importance on elevated routes that are built above streets and must therefore follow street curves and junctions.

Both longitudinal and lateral acceleration are limited by the tolerance of passengers rather than by technical factors. Various experiments have been conducted to assess the maximum rates of acceleration tolerable to both standing and seated passengers,[2, 13] and, in addition, operators have sometimes received indications of what passengers find acceptable. Passengers using the Paris Métro, for example, asked the operators to reduce the rates of acceleration used on their new rubber-tyre stock.

The maximum rates of acceleration normally found to be acceptable are as follows.

Autotaxi systems (all passengers seated)
Longitudinal and lateral: 2·5 m/s²

Autotram systems (passengers standing at times)
Longitudinal and lateral: 1·5 m/s²

71

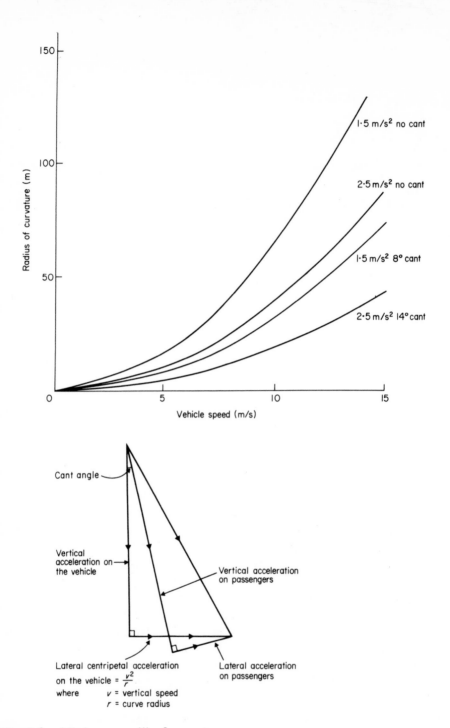

Fig. 5.8   Minimum radii of curvature

72

Jerk (the rate of change of acceleration) has been recognised as important for some years, but it has been found difficult to fix limits to its magnitude. Probably the most useful rule is that any change in rate of acceleration should take a minimum of 1 second to be completed.

Vertical accelerations (additional to gravity) are rarely critical in urban systems, but can be taken as having similar limitations to the other axes. Vehicles can be canted, which causes any lateral acceleration experienced by the vehicle to be felt by passengers as a reduced lateral acceleration with an additional vertical component, but difficulties can arise when vehicles stop on a canted curve, as passengers then experience an inwards acceleration equal to gravity multiplied by the sine of the cant angle. It is assumed in Fig. 5.8 that the maximum accelerations tolerable in this situation are the same as those previously mentioned. However, it could be argued that, as stopping on curves happens only in an emergency, the acceleration and the cant could be larger. Suspended vehicles that are free to swing could, in theory at least, travel round curves at such a high speed that the vertical acceleration on the passengers would become a limitation.

Notes

[1] The MIT results are discussed by SETEC Economie *et al.* in *Étude de systems pour un moyer de transport en commun discontinu en site propre*, EPALE, Cité administrative, 19 Étage, 59 Lille 1971.

[2] Urban Transport Technology Group, *Cabtrack Studies*, Royal Aircraft Establishment, Technical Report 68287, 1968.

[3] For example, the Télécanapé system built by the Habegger Company of Thun, Switzerland, and used at the Lausanne Fair in 1965.

[4] S.A. Driver, 'Design of railway rolling stock for heavy urban service', Paper 10 in *Rapid Transit Vehicles for City Services*, Institution of Mechanical Engineers, 1971.

[5] M.K. Eley *et al.*, *Cabtrack Studies*, Royal Aircraft Establishment, Technical Report 72047, 1972.

[6] F.T. Barwell's *Automation and Control in Transport* (Pergamon, 1973) gives details of steel-wheel, rubber-tyre and air-resistance systems. Data for air-cushion and magnetic-levitation systems have been estimated.

[7] H.E. Gramse *et al.*, *Noise and Vibration of a Steel Wheel/Steel Rail Personalized Rapid Transit System*, Transportation Systems Centre, Cambridge, Mass., UMTA MA 060027741, January 1974.

[8] F. Perrot, *The Flyda Study of Track Selection*, The Manor House, South Cerney, Cirencester, 1971.

[9] This is based on a qualitative judgement by members of the group who have heard the alternative methods of support in use.

[10] The Lectravia concept developed by Ling Temco Vought (LTV).

[11] M.K. Eley, *Cabtrack Studies*, Royal Aircraft Establishment, Technical Report 71188, 1971.

[12] R. Barnard and P.J. Rossignol, 'Practical problems in switching guidance and headway control of Minitram', *Control Aspects of New Forms of Guided Land Transport*, IEE Conference, 28–30 August 1974.

[13] T.W. Gibbard, *Acceleration and Comfort in Public Ground Transportation*, John Hopkins University, Silver Spring 1970.

6 Control

Automation of transport

Techniques for the self-regulation of such simple processes as heating a room are well developed, whereas the automation of company management or national government is far beyond human wit and, it is to be hoped, human desire. In any area of activity there is a threshold of complexity at which automatic control gives way to human control. The threshold has been moving slowly upwards during this century, propelled by technological advance and the rising real cost of labour. This process has been manifest in all forms of transport. The most extensively automated area of land passenger transport has been vertical movement within buildings; conversely, the control of road vehicles remains predominantly manual. The status of railway automation lies between these two extremes.

A lift is a relatively simple system: there is only one vehicle on the track, and that track is straight, very accurately aligned, under cover, and well protected from outside interference. By contrast, driving a bus in a city street is so complex as to be quite beyond the scope of present-day automatic equipment. The systems described in this book, while they may offer a service resembling that of a bus or taxi, run under conditions more akin to those of a lift. However, there are likely to be several vehicles on the same track, and the track will be curved, out-of-doors, built to modest standards of mechanical alignment, and prone to the occasional intrusion of such foreign bodies as leaves, rubbish, snow, and even people.

Passenger-transport systems have a number of features that distinguish them from most other devices to which automation is applied. The most significant of these are the importance attached to human safety, the complexity of the man—machine interface, the discontinuous nature of communication between the various parts, and the large number of independent variables.

Safety

Any new transport mode must have a level of safety that compares satisfactorily with that of existing modes. It will take much public discussion and some operating experience to decide whether it is the car, bus, train or lift that provides the appropriate standard. Any complex artefact is prone to failure: in transport that failure must generally entail no injury to passengers or staff. In railway circles, much is made of the concept known as 'fail-safe'. This means that any foreseeable component failure must lead directly to a safe state of system failure (for example, absence of an expected signal is to be treated as a stop signal). The list of such foreseeable failures has been compiled through 150 years of operating experience, occasionally tragic. The aviation industry — not having many forms of safe system failure available — has developed techniques of redundancy. Under redundant design, failure of a single component does not lead to system failure, safe or otherwise. The system is left in a weakened or more vulnerable state, and the broken component is repaired as soon as operationally possible.

Autotrams and autotaxis do not have the railway's wealth of operational experience. Nor, however, do they share the aircraft's vulnerability. So far, autotram control has been strongly influenced by fail-safe principles (as with LTV Airtrans, for example), while autotaxi control has employed more redundancy (as in the Demag-MBB Cabinentaxi). In almost all cases a safety monitoring system that is largely independent of normal running control is included, though there have been objections to this separation.[1]

Safety, reliability and service are linked at various levels. Low reliability of components will certainly cause poor service and probably reduce safety. High levels of safety can be obtained at the expense of service (by running very slowly) or at the expense of overall reliability (if the system is halted on the first signs of any irregularity). Redundant control helps to decouple safety and system reliability, but the duplication or triplication of components increases first cost and maintenance costs.

Interfaces

The man—machine information interface of a transport system has to contend with three sorts of people: passengers, who have to understand how the system works, communicate to it their particular needs, and receive from it advice and instructions (for example, 'Stand clear of the doors!'); the operating staff, who must monitor certain aspects of operation, be efficiently informed about failures, and have the means for exerting some direct control; and passers-by, including trespassers, who must be protected from injury and hence either warned out of danger or detected when moving into it.

At present, much public transport has poor communications either with its users or between its own staff, bus information being particularly poor. However, the control computers required for automation could also be used to improve information flows at interfaces. Already some railways have displays directly synchronised with train movements, and control centres for power stations and electrical transmission networks employ displays that are organised by computer. Some of these permit a dialogue between operator and data banks of a type directly applicable to fault monitoring in a transport network.

Detecting trespassers, fare-box thieves, and assaulters of elderly passengers is far less amenable to automation. Closed-circuit television, the assistance provided by other passengers and a few special detectors will be the norm for many years. Driverless transport will rarely develop into completely unstaffed transport.

Communication and control

A transport system may be modelled as a very large set of interacting variables. One might employ eight to describe a vehicle (position, speed, thrust, door position, temperature, load, destination, and safety status), four for each passenger (location in system, time since joining it, destination, and fare status), and a number of others for each station, junction, or length of track. Contemporary control theory and control technology are of only limited applicability to such multivariable systems, for they were largely developed in the different contexts of servo-mechanisms and chemical processes. Operations Research (OR) techniques, especially queueing theory, are of some help, but transport-network control requires a distinctive theory of its own, the development of which is still far from complete.

If the variables to be measured or controlled are grouped as above — according to whether they belong to vehicles, passengers, or stationary plant — the central rôle of communications is emphasised. Interactions between the latter two have already been mentioned under 'interfaces'. Transfer of data between vehicles and track, or between one vehicle and another, is expensive. Continuous contact is particularly difficult to maintain, and is therefore attempted only for certain categories of safety information. Most communication with vehicles is discontinuous, the availability of a link depending either on time or on vehicle position. These discontinuities have a considerable effect on the quality of regulation achievable, and on the way the control functions should be distributed between devices in different parts of the transport system.

Service patterns and their control requirements

A fleet of vehicles can be operated in various ways to provide a transport service. Although most of the interest in driverless urban transport is centred on autotram and autotaxi systems, many other configurations have been considered and some have been commercially developed. The principal patterns of service possible are described in this section, and are presented approximately in ascending order of control complexity.

Neverstops

A true neverstop is an extensive mechanism comprising a fleet of cars and a set of linkages, the whole driven by a stationary engine. The linkages are so designed that when the motor runs at a constant speed the cars undergo cyclic changes in speed. As each car passes a boarding point it travels very slowly and close to its neighbours; between boarding points both speed and spacing are increased. The time headway between vehicles, however, is kept constant. The linkages allow decelerating vehicles to transfer energy to accelerating ones, so that the drive motor provides power only to replace frictional losses. This motor, and hence the entire system, is regulated by a single controller; the very high inertia of the motor's load requires that starting up be executed with great care. Where the system is large, a number of motors may be used and their controllers suitably synchronised to ensure load sharing.

The price paid for control simplicity is complete operational rigidity: a neverstop has no means of absorbing temporary local disturbances, but runs or stops as an entity.

In recent years, some pseudo-neverstops, which provide the user with a pattern of service similar to that of the neverstop but do not employ mechanical linkages, have been constructed (e.g. Télécanapé in the Swiss Fair at Lausanne, 1965). In these, some simplicity of control is retained, but the advantages of a stationary drive and of energy transfers are lost.

Systems having one vehicle per track

If each track carries but one vehicle, inter-vehicle collisions are not possible. Lifts, funicular railways and aerial cableways are usually operated in this manner, their stationary motors being controlled so that cars move comfortably from one loading point to another. Where there are more than two such points, sequencing logic may be provided to tailor movements to passenger convenience. Indeed, in lift practice, elaborate algorithms have been devised for the efficient deployment of several vehicles on parallel tracks. Displays inform riding and intending passengers about the position of the car; push-buttons convey information from passengers to the control.

Two-speed AC motors or Ward-Leonard sets are operated to a set of speed, acceleration and jerk constraints. A wide variety of safety devices covers such conditions as overspeed, overrun, blocked doors and broken cables. High-resolution measuring devices are provided in the vicinity of stops to inform the motor controller of vehicle position: use of this information permits very accurate levelling to be performed, and floor misalignments are kept within a few millimetres.

In situations where track curvature makes cable hauling difficult, there is no reason why lift techniques should not be applied to a vehicle having its drive motor on board.

Stopping services

Most metros have an 'all-stops' service pattern, which makes them more amenable to automation than other sorts of railway. In the simplest configuration, the route contains no junctions, and longitudinal control is achieved by transmitting acceleration commands from trackside equipment to the vehicle. A set of such commands might comprise: 'motor', 'coast', 'brake' and 'brake hard'. Departure from stops may be based upon a predetermined schedule, or optimisation may be attempted to adapt schedules to actual service conditions.

Autotrams are usually designed to operate in an all-stops manner. They are much smaller than trains, and run at shorter headways. The control must therefore respond rapidly to emergencies, and needs also to be finer to give more precise stopping in stations. It is necessary to provide frequent opportunities for communication of data between vehicles and track. Efficient detectors of actual or incipient component failure are also necessary in the absence of a driver or guard.

Passengers need be provided with little information beyond a timetable, a map and some nameplates, unless the line is branched or short working (reversals prior to a terminus) is permitted. If it is, the control has to be more complex, to handle route selection, sequencing through junctions, reversing, and displays of service information.

Optional-stopping and skip-stop services

The time for a journey can be decreased by omitting some of the intermediate stops. If the vehicle is large, there will probably be passengers wishing to board or alight at every station. If it is small, this may not be so, and there is an advantage in making stopping dependent on demand, as in buses. Variable journey times are not compatible with exact schedules; if the service interval is short, the vehicles should be controlled to maintain even spacing rather than a fixed time. Optional-stopping services are particularly prone to bunching; this is best avoided by in some way regulating how many passengers board a particular vehicle. As with buses, channels of communication between passengers and the vehicle controller are required.

Instead of stopping on demand, vehicles can be scheduled to omit some stations along the line. Several distinct services must be interleaved to give complete journey cover — the more services there are, the greater the saving in journey time, but the longer the wait for a vehicle of the appropriate service to arrive. In this case, passengers need no longer communicate with vehicles, but should have instead an effective information display that is synchronised to vehicle movements.

Optional-stopping, and especially skip-stop, services benefit from the provision of passing places at some stations. These are expensive, and the merge and diverge junctions they entail require considerable elaboration of longitudinal control. However, their provision enables such patterns as 'express' and 'local' to be operated.

Autotaxis, simple and shared

Conventional taxis operate from a rank or may be called by telephone. Autotaxis employ a mixture of these styles: when a passenger enters a station, he may find an empty vehicle there, or he may have to wait while one is sent to him from a store or another station. Autotaxi stations are off-line, so that every journey starts with a merge manoeuvre onto the main line and terminates with a diverge manoeuvre. The network may contain many junctions. Economic considerations require high vehicle flow rates, and hence time headways as little as a second or two. There is thus a need for high-performance headway control, routing and merging control, the regulation of manoeuvres in stations, and the despatching of empty vehicles. The large number of vehicles may result in a significant incidence of breakdowns, so an efficient recovery procedure is also required.

As the network approaches saturation (during rush hours), intending passengers should be advised of their journey prospects via an interactive display. An autotaxi system should be less prone to congestion than a road-based system, for, when particular despatching or routing decisions are made, information about traffic in the whole network is available. However, the processing of such a mass of data requires a large computer, which is a normal adjunct to an autotaxi system.

Vehicle occupancy in a simple autotaxi system has been estimated to average about 1·4 passengers. Raising this figure by the organisation of vehicle sharing would increase line passenger capacity, or, alternatively (for a fixed capacity), would permit reduction of vehicle flow rates and, hence, an increase in time headways. Shared taxis may thus need a less critical headway-control system. However, the despatch procedure becomes much more complex. In the Morgantown installation there are few stations, and passenger sharing of entire journeys is intended. In a larger network this becomes impractical, for every station would be crowded with passengers for different destinations, all waiting for newcomers to bring their travel party up to a viable size. In such a network, taxi sharing must entail picking up or dropping off passengers *en route*. Techniques for the organisation of vehicle sharing have been developed for road-based 'dial-a-bus' services, but much work has yet to be done before they can be extended for use with autotaxis. Oom investigated the merits of autotaxi sharing in a design study for Gothenburg.[2]

Variable platoons

A transport system using large vehicles can have a large passenger capacity; one using small vehicles can offer a better service to fewer passengers. Various designers have sought to combine high capacity with good service by the use of platoons of small vehicles, individual vehicles joining or leaving a platoon at any station or junction. Unfortunately, although vehicles can be safely *detached* from the back of a moving platoon (cf. the 'slip coaches' once used by some railway companies), the *addition* of vehicles is generally hazardous. Fig. 6.1 shows how — for a given braking performance — the velocity with which one vehicle might strike the rear of another depends on their initial spacing and on the suddenness with which the leader decelerates. Curve (b) represents a possible design condition. Assuming impacts of up to 2m/s to be acceptable, safety requires initial spacing to lie outside the band 0·5 to 29m. Vehicles can be run singly at spacings greater than the latter figure, or in platoons at spacings less than the former. Conventional trains are assembled from coaches with no spacing. Any manoeuvre involving the formation or break up of a platoon travelling at speed must temporarily result in spacings lying within the danger band. Fig. 6.2 shows one proposed method of

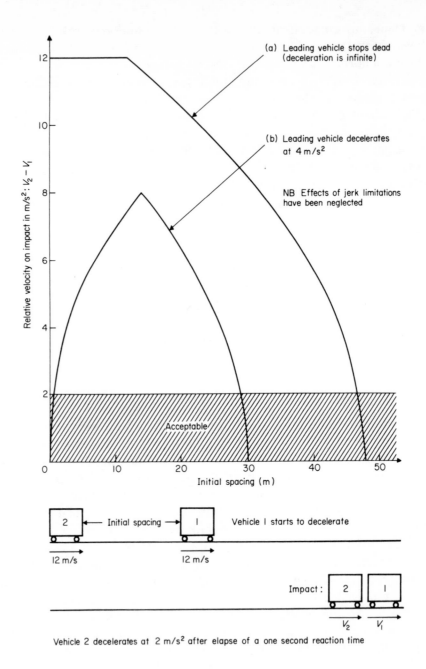

Fig. 6.1 Impact velocity following rapid deceleration of the leading vehicle of a pair

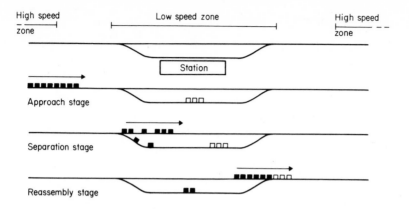

Fig. 6.2 Platoon reformation manoeuvre proposal for Matra 'Aramis' system

operating platoons having a variable make-up.

The problem of danger during platoon make-up can be tackled in three ways: by the use of low speed, use of special track, and adoption of a probabilistic safety criterion. Low-speed formation can be made safe, but may defeat the original objective of increasing capacity. The act of slowing down and speeding up again is associated with a loss in line capacity, which may cancel out the gain due to coupling vehicles. Higher-speed formation manoeuvres may be acceptable in particular places: certain stretches of surface-level straight track, having extra fencing and special control, may be deemed safe for vehicles having *any* spacing. Finally, all spacings can be regarded as hazardous to some degree, so that a safety criterion could be expressed in terms of the product of the degree of danger associated with a particular condition and the probability of that condition occurring. Under this philosophy, vehicle spacings having a high hazard rating may be acceptable provided their existence is but momentary. Debates about choice of safety criteria are ultimately resolved by experience in operation. For this reason, variable platoons are not likely to be employed *ab initio,* but rather as a development of an existing, simpler system.

The formation of platoons at speed may require some refinements to vehicle-following controllers, whereas formation of a stationary train can be achieved with conventional forms of longitudinal controller. Matra Aramis vehicles are intended to execute the former manoeuvre, Krauss-Maffei vehicles the latter.

Dual-mode and pallet systems

Guided transport is financially viable only when the guideway is intensively used. Most cities have a high density of movement near to the centre and a much lower density in the suburbs. In the United States, there has been interest in combining road-based suburban travel with guideway travel to the city centre. However, a vehicle suitable for both manual and automatic driving is likely to be complex, expensive, and may have to be maintained to a level of reliability incompatible with private ownership. For these and other reasons, dual-mode transport based on private cars has lost favour. There remains the possibility of operating a suburban bus that can run onto a guideway (at which point the driver gets out and automatic control takes over). The viability of such an arrangement is strongly dependent on the relative lengths of the distribution (road) and corridor (track) portions of a typical journey.

To simplify the design of dual-mode vehicles, the use of carriers is sometimes proposed. Such carriers are essentially motorised chassis for automatic operation on a guideway, and convey road vehicles in much the same way as certain railway trucks do. Unfortunately, even a small bus, when mounted on a carrier, requires a guideway with a wastefully large loading gauge. No special control techniques beyond those already mentioned are required.

Distribution of control tasks

The activities to be controlled in an autotaxi or autotram system are numerous. Table 6.1 gives some indication of their extent. The designer of such a system must not only decide which of these activities are to be fully automated, but must also choose a control structure. The different regulatory tasks have to be assigned to specific devices in the vehicles, at the trackside or in a central control room. The assignment should attempt to minimise cost, ensure a reasonable level of reliability, localise the influence of breakdowns, and simplify the proving of the control system when first installed. As these aims conflict with each other, compromise is required.

Communication links contribute substantially to both cost and un-reliability. Some links are essential — e.g. for safety — whilst others improve the level of service that can be offered. It is sometimes possible to devise control systems that degrade gently as non-essential, but helpful, information is lost. The term 'fail-soft' has been used for this desirable

Table 6.1

Activities requiring control in an automatic transit system

Automatically controlled	Vehicle guidance and suspension (if of active type) Longitudinal motion, including manoeuvres in stations and at junctions Sequencing vehicles through a merge Operation of switches or points Operation of doors, station lifts and escalators, barriers Heating or air-conditioning Fare collection (ultimate cash collection may be manual)
Automatically and/or manually controlled	Despatch of vehicles from termini or stores Marshalling vehicles in storage areas Generation of routes and schedules Handling service or timetable inquiries Removal of defective vehicles from track Testing vehicles, inspection of track Stopping and restarting the whole system Battery charging, etc.
Manually controlled	Track and vehicle maintenance Crime and vandalism Cleaning

property. A 'fail-hard' system, which works well or not at all, is considerably easier to design but ill suited to public transport.

A well-developed approach to the control of complex systems, and one that is compatible with the fail-soft objective, is shown in Fig. 6.3. The diagram has a familiar form; however, it must be remembered that in automation there are no *informal* lateral links to back up the vertical ones. Level 1 deals with the local and immediate: here communication failures cause correspondingly immediate, but local, disruption. Level 3 communicates, but infrequently, with the level 2 controllers below it. Provided that these possess some means of storing their objectives, the links at the top of the diagram could be severed for long periods without complete breakdown of the system. However, while such a severance persists, the general system performance would gradually decline. Level 3 activities in transportation include control of fleet distribution and alleviation of congestion.

Pure hierarchical control is not particularly suited to driverless

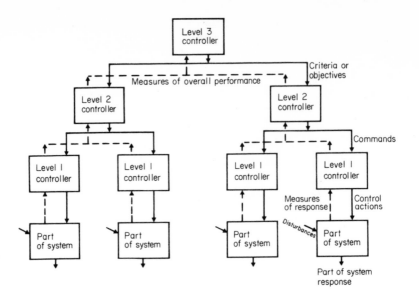

Fig. 6.3   Hierarchical control in its most fundamental form

transport. Level 1 corresponds to vehicle control and level 2 to track-sector regulation. A given vehicle passes through many different sectors. However, a hierarchical system of some sort is needed if a failure in one vehicle is not to propagate backwards through the entire network.

Fig. 6.4 shows a number of control hierarchies. The single-tier arrangement, well known to car drivers, is unworkable with driverless vehicles. A centralised two-tier design is very expensive as regards communication links: it is practical to duplicate a central control computer, but not the entire network of long links to vehicles. Localised two-tier control is quite feasible and is appropriate for some autotrams. A three-tier system has generally been chosen for autotaxis. Where a quasi-independent safety-supervision system is used parallel with normal operating control, it is not necessary that both should have the same structure. A single-tier collision-avoidance monitor is compatible with multi-tier control.

Whichever hierarchy is chosen, the changing physical structure (as vehicles move along) must be accommodated by the control. One technique for this is to create lateral communication links in addition to the vertical ones. In a three-tier structure, the intermediate tier of local controllers could pass on information before a vehicle crosses from one controllers' zone of influence into another's. Alternatively, communication

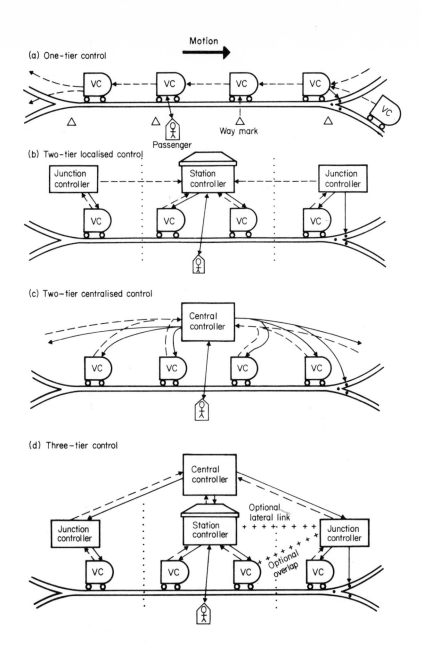

Fig. 6.4   Different control hierarchies

Solid lines denote commands; broken lines denote measurements
VC = vehicle controller; dotted lines denote control area boundaries

links can be duplicated in an overlap section, so that vehicles passing from one zone to another are known to the controllers of both. Neither of these provisions have been made explicit in the published descriptions of three-tier autotaxi-control.[3] In their absence, the central controller must act as a telephone exchange for information exchanged between the lower tiers.

Longitudinal control criteria

The control of any transport system has objectives that may be classified under the headings: cost, comfort, safety, speed, capacity, and accuracy. The regulation of the motion of any particular vehicle along its track has objectives derived from those of the system as a whole.

Providing for communication and control will absorb a substantial part of the total capital cost of an automated system — from 10 to 40 per cent according to the degree of novelty and sophistication. Within control, the separate functions of measurement, communication, data-processing and actuation will involve comparable expense. Moreover, the development and testing of the control algorithms may well cost as much as the physical devices to carry out (in computer jargon, the software may cost as much as the hardware). Long-term research into advanced techniques of automation is underway in several countries; however, the immediate task of system developers is to devise reliable equipment for performing the basic functions. The control of autotaxis is much more difficult than that of autotrams, and there must be considerable doubt about whether it is wise to attempt the former before gaining operational experience of the latter. In general terms, autotaxis require closer headways and more complex despatching. The former directly increases the cost of measurement and communication in longitudinal control.

Comfort is a quality that is difficult to measure. It has a psychological component that is concerned with freedom from fear, and a physiological component that is related to such measurable entities as temperature, noise and motion. As far as longitudinal control is concerned, the acceleration and jerk applied to passengers should be low or infrequent. Limits of $2 \cdot 5$ m/s^2 for seated passengers and $1 \cdot 5$ m/s^2 for standing passengers were mentioned in Chapter 5, as was a minimum time of 1 second for the application or removal of these accelerations. The use of limits is a primitive way of controlling acceleration, and more sophisticated techniques exist. However, limits are easy to apply during controller design. If higher accelerations were acceptable during normal running, journey times could be reduced; if higher rates of emergency braking were allowed, capacity could be expanded. Some existing vehicles are uncomfortable not because acceleration or jerk reach excessive values, but because they are constantly fluctuating. Good longitudinal control should suppress these fluctuations.

Safety impinges primarily upon longitudinal control — the prospect of a vehicle 'out of control' is a daunting one. Normal running must be safe; abnormal running must be both detected and corrected. Assuring the former requires a thorough and imaginative rehearsal of all possible configurations that the system could assume, and the removal from the operational repertoire of any that entail danger. The specification of failure detectors follows an analysis of failure modes — probably the most difficult stage in the design of a control scheme. Detectors are necessary for *inter alia* overspeeding, premature opening of doors, reverse motion, fire, and approaching another vehicle too closely. The time available to correct an abnormality depends on the promptness of detection and on vehicle spacing. Safety thus determines the minimum frequency at which detector outputs should be sampled, and in the case of autotaxis defines the minimum usable headway. For certain sorts of abnormality, emergency braking at, say, 5 m/s^2 is an appropriate response, passenger discomfort being acceptable as an alternative to possible injury. The simplest forms of emergency brake do not, unfortunately, give accurately predictable stopping patterns, the decelerations obtained varying with gradient, weather conditions, wear since last adjustment, and the number of passengers in a vehicle. The guaranteed retardation rate may be as low as 40 per cent of the maximum possible.[4] More complex brakes designed to give constant decelerations could subject passengers to injuriously high forces if they were to fail into a full-on state. One possible design for reliable yet safe emergency braking has two sets of brakes acting in parallel.

Increasing vehicle speed will require intensification of the safety restrictions — for example, the increasing of headways. Higher speed requires the provision of larger motors and electrical gear, increases the specific fuel consumption, and may shorten vehicle life. However, few travellers actually want slow motion, whilst an operator can use a smaller vehicle fleet to move a given number of passengers if speeds are raised. The interaction of the track curvature (necessary to fit a new system into the existing urban fabric) and passenger comfort often acts as the most severe constraint on speed. Autotrams and autotaxis generally employ a maximum velocity in the range of 10 to 16 m/s.

The *capacity* of a transport system is the level of demand at which the service becomes intolerable. The vehicular capacity of a link is the reciprocal of the minimum time headway between vehicles. This latter is determined by emergency stopping distance, loading time in a station, or some combination of the two. The two examples below indicate typical headways for autotaxi and autotram systems.

Example 1. Autotaxi headway can be based on the principle of spacing vehicles so that, no matter what happens to the vehicle ahead, any following vehicle can be brought to a halt without touching it ('brick-wall' stop criterion). If emergency braking takes 0·5s to apply and causes a deceleration of 5 m/s^2, vehicle length is 3m and another 3m is allowed as reaction distance, then the figures below obtain.

Case   (i): all vehicles travel at 12 m/s. Headway must exceed 1·9s, giving a nominal link capacity of 1,900 vehicles per hour.

Case (ii): all vehicles travel at 6 m/s. Headway must exceed 1·77s, giving a nominal link capacity of 2,030 vehicles per hour.

Case (iii): all vehicles pass from a high-speed section (12m/s) to a low speed section (6 m/s) by means of a manoeuvre to the comfort limits of $a = 2·5$ m/s^2 and $j = 2·5$ m/s^3, where a is acceleration and j is jerk. Safety conditions are met throughout the manoeuvre. Headway must exceed 2·5s, giving a nominal link capacity of 1,440 vehicles per hour.

Example 2. Autotram headway can be based on the principle of vehicles never approaching within their own length (5m) of each other while following through a station. Dwell time is 10s, and starting and stopping are carried out with an acceleration of 1·5m/s^2 and jerk of 1·5m/s^3.

Headway must exceed 16·2s, giving a nominal link capacity of 222 vehicles per hour (this headway corresponds to 194m at a full speed of 12m/s, which is several times the relevant emergency stopping distance of 54m).

The above examples show the expected difference between autotaxi and autotram link capacities. More specifically, the first shows the deleterious influence on capacity of certain sorts of speed change, and hence the need for especially careful control during them. The second example shows that the *effective* dwell time in a station is significantly greater than the actual stop time, because vehicles need time to clear their own length before others can take their place. There are control techniques for increasing mean station throughput, but they require that vehicles run at uneven spacing.

Accuracy was the last item on the list of objectives given above. With good feedback control, the speeds, accelerations and jerks can be kept close to their declared limits, and travel times can be kept close to their minimum. Accurate stopping in stations speeds the transfer of passengers. Reliability of arrival time is particularly useful in a scheduled service.

Longitudinal control techniques

Each vehicle should move at the lowest of three speeds: the nominal speed, the safe following speed, and the comfortable trajectory speed. The first is a value assigned to every portion of track after taking into account curvature, gradient and fuel economy. The second depends on the safety criterion employed, in conjunction with the distance to the vehicle ahead. The third is the speed that will give a comfortable trajectory to the next stopping point. Key parameters are, therefore: nominal speed, vehicle speed, distance to vehicle ahead, and distance to scheduled stopping point. The first of these does not normally vary with time, but the others do and must be measured. Two further measurements that can improve the quality of longitudinal control are the acceleration of own vehicle and the velocity of the vehicle ahead.

Information about a vehicle's velocity or acceleration is readily available on-board the vehicle in question, but can only with some difficulty be obtained directly from the trackside. Conversely, position is more easily determined from the trackside, although a few vehicle-borne ranging devices have been developed for use over short distances. Nominal speeds, once calculated, are readily stored by trackside equipment, whereas their storage in a vehicle's memory entails a rather complex process of interpretation according to vehicle position.

Two approaches to longitudinal control may be distinguished, and can be called on-vehicle control and trackside control respectively. In the former, most of the decision-making takes place on-board the vehicle, which must therefore be supplied with the appropriate measurements. In the latter, the vehicle receives commands from a trackside decision-making device. In either case there will be communication (of measurements or commands) between vehicle and track, and the nature of this communication process has a strong influence on the quality of control.

Most information passed from trackside equipment must be directed to a particular vehicle. An expensive solution to this problem is to employ a general broadcast to all vehicles, with messages prefaced by a call sign identifying the vehicle concerned (exceptionally, each vehicle could have its own carrier frequency). A simpler solution is to provide a separate communication channel to each section of track, the sections being short enough never to carry more than one vehicle. Clearly, the sections must be particularly short in stations or before junctions, where it may be necessary to queue vehicles. Under trackside control, the messages are commands that are peculiar to each vehicle; hence, the routing of messages to track sections must be kept synchronised with the movements of the vehicles. Under on-vehicle control, the messages sent to a particular section are measurements (independent of which vehicle is in the section) and a simpler routing scheme suffices. A third solution to the message routing problem is to employ alterable signboards at intervals along the track. The vehicle reads each one as it passes by (conventional railway signals, while superficially of this type, have long sighting distances and are more akin to the sectioned communications just discussed). The vehicle must remember the message until it reaches the next board, by which time some of the earlier information may be stale. Of course, the vehicle must not come to a stop between boards!

All the comments in the previous paragraph apply as much to vehicle-to-track as to track-to-vehicle communication. In practice, a mixture of message routing techniques can be employed. Signboards are suitable for transmitting the local value of nominal speed: emergency braking commands require broadcast or section treatment.

The actual path of communication can be through the running rails (if present); through special signal rails, with which the vehicle maintains contact by means of brushes; or through space itself, using light or magnetic induction. Optical links are not very reliable, but electrical and magnetic links are used in a variety of forms. Signals sent through an electrical path are subject to interference from adjacent power circuits and are therefore transmitted in coded or modulated form. Signals coupled magnetically into vehicle receivers must in addition lie in a frequency range giving efficient coupling. Two popular forms of magnetic coupling are those employing loops of wire in the track or lossy coaxial cables.[5] Transponders (which respond to interrogation by a coded signal) have been developed for road and railway use and could be used as signboards in automated systems.

On-vehicle control

Basic form. The simplest form of on-vehicle control applicable to autotrams is an extension of railway practice. Own velocity and acceleration are measured on board each vehicle, and the limits of passenger tolerance to jerk and acceleration are incorporated directly into the controller design. Nominal speed and the distance to the next stopping place are displayed on signboards, which are 'read' by passing vehicles. Between boards, the value read for the latter is corrected by subtracting the distance travelled since passing the last board (e.g. as measured by counting wheel revolutions). Distance to the vehicle ahead is expressed as a number of blocks and electronically communicated by trackside signals of the sector or signboard types. However, the velocity of the vehicle ahead is not measured directly, nor can it be construed with any accuracy from the block signalling.

Limitations. This basic control form is rather unsatisfactory for certain manoeuvres, and for achieving high capacities.

Every time a vehicle encounters a drop in nominal speed at a point remote from a scheduled stop, it is likely to find itself travelling too fast. A large drop such as this would induce emergency braking. Consequently, any such drops should be communicated as a series of small downward steps.

Where a number of vehicles travel close together over a considerable distance, platoon instability can occur. Any disturbance to the speed of the first vehicle may be so multiplied by the cascaded control action of those that follow, that the last vehicle undergoes wild fluctuations in speed. Block signalling used in conjunction with highly responsive vehicle controllers results in such instability. The simple cure of reducing controller responsiveness unfortunately also reduces the efficiency with which other manoeuvres (such as formation of a vehicle queue) can be performed. Platoon instability of this type need not however cause concern in most autotram applications, since the close spacing of stations prevents the formation of large platoons.

Compared to an ideal vehicle ranging system, fixed-block signalling gives a low line capacity. Uncertainty as to the location of a vehicle within a block requires vehicles to be run at a greater spacing than they would if headway were known more accurately. Headways of approximately stopping distance plus one block length must be employed. Thus, the smaller the block length, the smaller the working headway and the greater the capacity. Unfortunately, reducing block length also raises the cost of signalling.

It is desirable that vehicles should be able to stop accurately, quickly and smoothly. The designers of lifts have made a particular study of ways of performing this manoeuvre and have devised some elegant non-linear control laws for the purpose. One such law makes speed proportional to the square root of the distance to the stopping point. However, it is unlikely that information from signboards would be sufficiently accurate for use with these laws.

Refinements. The limitations of basic on-vehicle control do not preclude its use for autotrams, but for autotaxis some refinements are desirable. Distance to the vehicle ahead and to the next stopping point should be measured with a fine resolution, particularly when they are small. Several devices have been developed for this purpose. Nominal speed information must be transmitted to vehicles in such a way that they can interpolate smoothly between one value and the next.

Platoon instability is avoidable if vehicles have early intimation of the commencement of manoeuvres by vehicles ahead of them. One form of such information is a measure of the velocity of the vehicle ahead. Fig. 6.5 shows how a significant change in relative velocity develops well before a significant change in headway, 5 per cent of the operational value of these quantities being taken as 'significant' in each case. Knowledge of leading vehicle acceleration would be even more useful (car drivers are much assisted by the provision of brake lights in the vehicle ahead). However, only devices for measuring relative velocity have been developed to date.

Trackside control

The commands from a trackside controller to a vehicle may specify thrust (or acceleration), speed or position. In all cases, it is convenient to apply limits to acceleration and jerk by modifying the commands after they reach the vehicle.

Thrust commands. Thrust depends on motor current and brake setting, and is related to acceleration via vehicle mass, track gradient, and other variable factors. It is therefore desirable to employ closed-loop motor control to a commanded acceleration rather than direct command thrust. A trackside controller, noting the times at which a vehicle passes a number of checkpoints, can issue acceleration commands to it. However, even with closely-spaced checkpoints the method gives poor results. It is satisfactory for speeding up a vehicle from rest and for braking it to rest again in an emergency, but it is not satisfactory for running at short headways or for stopping accurately at a station. A form of mixed thrust and speed control has been used for several decades on the Post Office underground mailbag railway in London; however, on that system predictability of transit time is not important.

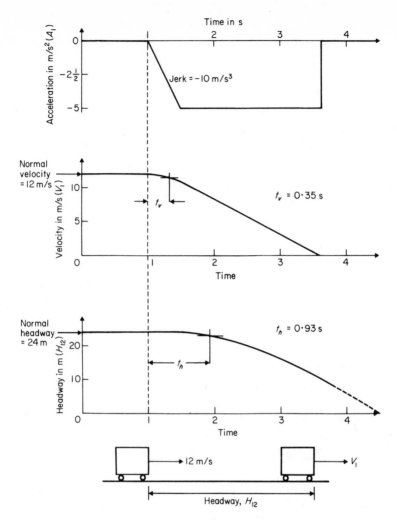

Fig. 6.5   Violent deceleration of leading vehicle
t_v is time for velocity to fall by 5 per cent
t_h is time for position headway to fall by 5 per cent

Velocity commands. Better control results if velocity is specified. The velocity commands are often not vehicle-specific, and can therefore be easily communicated on a section-by-section basis. Vehicle following is satisfactory provided position measurements are made with a fine resolution. Stopping accurately at a station or in a queue is more difficult and requires that the communication sections be very short. If they are not, stopping is likely to entail a series of slow lurches. Under velocity control, the longer the journey the more uncertain the time of arrival at a destination.

Position commands. This is not so if position commands are transmitted to each vehicle. Under such a scheme, each vehicle also needs a direct measure of where it is (closely-spaced track markers are usually installed for this purpose). The desired position changes continuously as the vehicle moves, so position commands must be frequently updated. The most widely used form of trackside position control is known variously as marker-following, or synchronous or moving-slot control. A train of pulses is broadcast to most of the vehicles in a network, each pulse being interpreted as a command to advance by one track marker. The marker spacing is varied from place to place in order to define the normal speed for each length of track (speed = marker spacing x pulse rate). Switching on extra track markers in front of a particular vehicle will cause it to slow down, but it can only be completely stopped by removing the pulse train. Each vehicle has a tolerance zone around its commanded position; deviations outside this zone are interpreted as some form of failure and lead to following vehicles being brought to a halt.

Marker following is a simple way of organising each vehicle to follow the same speed—position trajectory. It handles the close spacing situation without causing platoon instability, though an extra headway allowance is required to accommodate the tolerance zone mentioned above. Conflicts between marker-following vehicles at merges are fairly easy to resolve. Stopping and queueing are not so easy, as variations in the marker positions and the pulse rate may have to be made between one vehicle and its successor.

An extreme form of marker following was proposed and part-tested for Cabtrack.[6] Here vehicles were to travel at spacings less than their stopping distance and the commanded positions were interpreted as where vehicles should stop if no further instructions were received. Thus, vehicles ran behind their moving markers by an amount that increased with speed. Marker following is used at Morgantown,[3] but continental autotaxi designers appear to prefer on-vehicle to trackside control.

Longitudinal control, whether of vehicle or trackside form, is generally backed by a safety monitoring system. This should not only confirm that commands are obeyed and measurements received, but also directly test that vehicle configurations are safe. The rare emergency commands must overrule all others.

Some of the basic facets of longitudinal control are still not well understood — really efficient yet practical junction and coupling manoeuvres have yet to be developed. The recent growth in emphasis on autotram at the expense of autotaxi has been reflected in the greater interest in the simplest forms of automatic control, particularly those nearest to railway practice.

Routing and despatching

As was discussed in Chapter 5, the switching mechanism that routes a vehicle at a fork can be located in the track or mounted on the vehicle. The operation of the mechanism must be integrated with the longitudinal control system to ensure safe and smooth motion through the fork. The decision as to which branch the mechanism should select can be treated in a variety of ways, of which the principal ones can be labelled stored route, stored destination, and vehicle identity. These are discussed below.

On starting a journey, a vehicle can be advised of its route as a sequence of left or right branches. As it travels along, it identifies each fork that it encounters and consults its internal store for the appropriate instruction. The vehicle thus requires a logical processor and a memory that is periodically recharged. The technique is prone to error – one wrong turn and the vehicle is completely lost – and it is inflexible. It is also difficult to modify a route to avoid a link blocked by congestion or breakdown. However, stored route may be employed on a very simple network carrying autotrams.

Alternatively, each vehicle can carry the name of its destination. On approaching a junction this is read by the local controller there and compared with a list to yield the relevant route. A variant of this method is for the junction to present the vehicle with a signpost that enables it to translate its destination into a switching decision. However, this variant entails a more voluminous data transfer. Both versions are flexible, as the list or signpost can be modified in response to operational conditions. Moreover, a mistake at any one junction will be automatically rectified at the next. In autotaxi operations there may even be occasions when it would be preferable to mis-route a vehicle rather than have it wait for the shortest route to become clear. This sort of decision is readily incorporated into the routing list of a junction controller.

Vehicle identity can be read from a suitable coded board carried by each vehicle. Optical, magnetic or other forms of coding can be used and, as the identity number need never be altered, the board can be made robust. The vehicle requires no decision-making device, but the junction controller must have advance information concerning what to do with each vehicle. Communication is required either with the controllers of adjacent stations and junctions or with a central computer, as loss of communication means loss of ability to perform routing.

Routing is concerned with forks. Merges are the bottlenecks of a system and require special attention. Sometimes forks and merges are so closely associated in an intersection that the same local controller has to handle both routing and sequencing.

Two broad strategies are available for resolving conflicts at merges: the deterministic and the stochastic.

Deterministic merge control is compatible only with trackside longitudinal control employing position commands (e.g. marker following). It also requires the participation of a central computer in every despatch decision. Where the future position of every despatched vehicle is calculable, it is possible to restrict the moment a journey begins to one at which a conflict-free path can be guaranteed. Queueing at a merge point somewhere in the course of a journey is replaced by a delay in journey departure. To implement deterministic junction control, it is necessary to have a reservation table covering every potential bottleneck in the network; route and despatch time are chosen after searching this table. There is some evidence that an autotaxi system using this form of control can attain higher capacities than under stochastic control. This is offset by the greater vulnerability of deterministic control to component failures.

Stochastic merge control is, by contrast, an activity localised in time and space. Each junction controller notes which vehicles are entering its zone of influence and delays each one sufficiently to ensure that it reaches the merge point without conflict. If the merge is overloaded a queue forms, and this eventually backs up into the zone of an upstream controller. Communications between a central controller and one regulating a junction are largely of a statistical nature − information about actual or expected vehicle flow rates and about mean delays. The essence of stochastic control is that specific information about vehicles arriving in the future is not available. While stochastic control is usually equated with local control, this is not essential. An algorithm in a central computer can exercise control of one junction without detailed reference to what is happening at the others.

Much research has been undertaken on linking road traffic signals together and rather less on the mutual interactions of railway junctions. Autotram will rarely need complex junction control, but autotaxi may yet adopt techniques from other fields. For autotram, an area being more urgently developed is the management of a timetable. There are as yet few known Operations Research techniques suitable for the generation of timetables, and few control strategies for maximising service standard in the face of unpredictable passenger loading. Some simple examples of the latter have been tried with metros and buses but without marked success. Phenomena such as bunching are more likely to affect autotrams than systems employing large vehicles.

Notes

[1] P.D. Thomas and J. Hopkinson, 'A longitudinal control strategy derived from the basic safety constraint', *Control Aspects of New Forms of Guided Land Transport* (CNFT), IEE Conference Publication no. 117, London, August 1974.

[2] R. Oom, 'The case for small vehicles', in I.G. Black *et al, Advanced Transport in British Cities,* Urban Transport Research Group, University of Warwick, 1974.

[3] For example, V.E. Hutton and S. Berry, 'Morgantown personal rapid transit control and communication system', *Bendix Technical Journal,* vol. 16, no. 1, pp. 17–25, Spring 1973.

[4] E.J. Hinman and G.L. Pitts, 'Practical headway limitations for personalised automated transit systems', CNFT, op.cit.

[5] B.W. Hutchings and D.J. Cree, 'Longitudinal track to vehicle communications', CNFT, op.cit.

[6] Royal Aircraft Establishment Urban Transport Group, *Cabtrack Studies,* RAE Technical Report 68287, parts 1 and 2, 1968.

7 Economic Assessment

The concern of this chapter is with the allocation of economic resources and both problems of design and evaluation are examined. The design objective is to provide a service that fits as closely as possible the needs and values of the passengers; it is a service that contains the right balance between comfort and cost (which affects vehicle size), between walking and faster journey speeds (which affects station spacing), and between waiting time and cost (which affects vehicle size and the sophistication of the control equipment). These conflicts and many others need to be resolved before we can say 'That is the best automated transport can offer here' and go on to the evaluation stage to decide whether the system is justified on economic grounds.

The purpose of evaluation is to compare the effects of taking one course of action — in this case the construction of a transport route served by automated vehicles — with an alternative, and to decide which is the best choice. If the correct conclusion is to be reached, the alternatives must be described accurately, and the best (or, at least, near to the best) options available for each taken into account. They should not just be pale imitations, nor, necessarily, simple projections of the present. In a sense, the evaluation process can also be considered as part of a wider design problem; that is, the design of a transport system for an urban area, and an attempt to find those routes and areas where automated transport ought to be used in preference to other transport. This involves a consideration of the advantages and disadvantages of different forms of transport (foot, pedal, motor — public and private) and an attempt to integrate them into a complete transport system for the urban area.

This view of design and evaluation represents an oversimplification and evades a number of practical difficulties. Although representing design as an optimisation problem may clarify certain issues, its formal definition and solution is far from straightforward in most cases. The difficulty of defining accurately all the economic and social relationships, the complexity of many of the technological relationships, and the idiosyncratic nature of urban areas forces us to fall back on *ad hoc* and partial methods of analysis. Eventually, by trial and error, we may arrive at a point near the optimum, though, especially when dealing with new technology, we should remember that costs and people's values will almost certainly change over time as conditions change and more information becomes available. Furthermore, when forecasting, we should remember that naïve projections of conventional or existing technology may give an unfair representation of their potential and optimum rôle in the future. For instance, in recent years, people's conception of the rôle of buses and public transport has been changing rapidly and will no doubt change further before the end of the decade. We should beware of any assumptions that the rôle of the bus will be the same in the 1980s and 1990s as it was in the 1960s or early 1970s.

A problem associated with appraisal is the definition of boundaries beyond which the impact of the subject under study is so small as to be of no significance. The decision on where to stop the analysis is a difficult one. It partly rests on the resources available to the analyst and the often limited information available to him about second- or third-order effects. In the appraisal of new technology, this problem is likely to be magnified by the absence of any previous experience of the product or service. New and unanticipated effects may occur after the introduction of a new product, or people's appreciation of it may differ radically from that anticipated prior to its introduction.

An appraisal of a new transport mode can, at one level, just examine its impact on passenger movement, assuming all other things remain constant. But, of course, many other things will not remain constant: bus operation will be curtailed to avoid duplication with the new mode; the pattern or scale of road investment may change; and even the pattern of land use — residential density, the location of employment, and so on — may change with the appearance of the new mode. All of these reactions are difficult to forecast with any confidence. We have not examined in detail the effect of a new transport mode on land use mainly because we did not believe the effect would be large (over a period of 10 to 20 years, anyway), though it must be admitted that this was partly also because we know of no suitable techniques for adequately modelling such a process and evaluating its results.

Recognising these practical and theoretical difficulties of finding the exact rôle autotram should play in cities of the future, we decided to concentrate on examining autotram in a specific setting and then project these results to other settings, both in other cities and at different periods in the future.

The scenario we chose to examine was Coventry in 1981. The primary reason for this choice was the completion in 1972 of the Coventry Transportation Study, which examined in detail the transport prospects for the city in 1981. Using information and data from this source, we

102

examined the implications of installing an autotram route in Coventry. The study was intended to provide a broad assessment of the prospects for autotram in Coventry, and was not a detailed design study of all the problems that must be solved before a system could be built. We were interested in identifying the major features of an installation that are critical to its future adoption and success.

The following sections examine the economic aspects of autotram in Coventry: the change in transport costs and benefits to the people of Coventry and the surrounding districts that results from its introduction. Chapter 8 considers the environmental aspects of an autotram installation.

Coventry

Coventry is expected to have a population of 359,000 in 1981. If real incomes rise as expected during the 1970s (at a rate of 3 per cent per year), a substantial increase in car ownership and passenger journeys is forecast. During the peak period 1530–1800 hours 'person journeys' to, from and within the city are expected to rise from 165,000 in 1967 to 258,000 in 1981 – an average rise per year of 3·2 per cent.[1]

Examining the implication of this increase in demand, the Transportation Study Group first of all assumed there was no investment in the road network after 1976 and no restraint on the use of cars. The analysis clearly showed that the decline during the 1960s in the number of trips that occurred on public transport would continue during the 1970s. The projection of a drop from 50,500 to 38,900 in trips to, from or within the city during the 14-year period (see Table 7.1) represents an average fall of nearly 2 per cent per year. The fall in public transport trips (including education trips) is slightly less. This reflects both an increase in the number of people in full-time education and the use of larger educational units, which leads to longer journeys and a tendency to use public transport instead of walking.

For public transport in Coventry, therefore, the 'natural' demand situation (as the result of a no-restraint policy is called) seems bleak – the decline experienced during the 1960s would continue up to 1981, and presumably beyond. But, as the study pointed out, 'it was obvious that the road system would not cope with the natural demand' and 'if traffic is to be kept moving there will be a need to restrain the use of the private car'. The report then stated that if the City Council wished to impose some level of restraint on the private car 'it could . . . regulate demand through its pricing structure in various car parks', or, if this was not

Table 7.1

Person journeys by public transport, weekday, 1530–1800 hours

		Excluding education			Including education		
		1967	1981 (natural)	1981 (base)	1967	1981 (natural)	1981 (base)
1	City to city	41,700	30,900	50,400	53,400	47,300	66,800
2	City to surrounding county	5,800	5,600	12,700	6,000	5,800	12,900
3	County to city	3,000	2,400	1,800	3,500	2,700	2,100
4	1 + 2 + 3	50,500	38,900	64,900	62,900	55,800	81,800

Source: *The Coventry Transportation Study.*

possible, 'through the imposition of a limit on the number of car parking spaces.' Whichever method of restraint is used, it is expected to result in a substantial increase in the number of people using public transport and, as a result of the policy of restraint adopted by the study team, the prospect of a fall in trips by public transport is turned into a rise (see Table 7.1). It might be added here that 'it was apparent from the early results that the demand for private vehicle travel was insensitive to changes in the public transport service'.[2] Zero fares on public transport were examined and found to increase the demand for public transport trips (excluding education trips) from 38,900, to 52,300 in 1981.[3]

Two important riders ought to be added to the above forecasts. First, the large increase in the price of oil in 1973 (after the completion of the study) can be expected to change the course and balance of transport demand over the years ahead. The effect of this increase in price, if maintained (the price to be charged for North Sea oil is still an open question), would be to slow the rate of growth of private vehicle use and hence delay the need for restraint. Secondly, and perhaps more seriously, this forecast or base strategy (as it is called) is open to question on what exactly the level of restraint represents: whether it is the optimum level of restraint (i.e. a recommendation) or the likely outcome of political wrangling (and hence a forecast), or neither.

The study team, having established a base strategy, then went on to consider how transport investment funds should be allocated during the period 1976–81. Three major road options were considered, together with two public transport options (including a railway link between Coventry and Nuneaton). Two of the road schemes gave high first-year rates of return on capital investment (in the region of 25 per cent) and one of these was eventually chosen by the City Council. The public transport schemes were small variations on the traditional form of radial and occasional circumferential services. A modest expansion in commuter buses (i.e. fast with infrequent stops) and bus priority measures was considered desirable. Even after the construction of new roads restraint on the motorist would need to be maintained.

Methodology

In the UK during the last decade, a transport planning framework has been developed by central and local authorities together with commercial consultants and academics interested in transport. An important component of this framework is the transportation model. The purpose of the model is to describe the movement of people and vehicles on the transport network in the area that is being studied. The effect of changing the network by adding new roads or public transport routes, or by changing certain parameters (e.g. parking charges or public transport subsidies) can then be simulated. Following this, the result of any changes can be compared with the initial situation, with a view to forming an opinion on the merits of the change. This comparison can be in the form of a cost-benefit analysis, in which all the costs and benefits of the change are tabulated, converted to the common unit of money, and a figure, which may be either positive or negative, derived for the balance of benefits minus costs (net benefit).

The transportation model

In the study of autotram in Coventry, the methods used for modelling transport movement closely follow those recommended by the Department of the Environment and used in the Coventry Transportation Study. Data and parameters from the study were also used as a basis for our own simulations. Numerous criticisms have been levelled at these techniques — both at their inadequacies in representing transport movement, and at their ability to represent the transport opportunities available in urban areas. There is undoubtedly room for improvement, and it can be anticipated that there will be considerable refinements in the future. Our justification for adopting these techniques is that they represent an explicit set of modelling techniques comprehensible to many transport planners (in the UK at least), and a procedure (we hope, refined and improved) that any future evaluation of autotram will necessarily have to follow closely.

Fig. 7.1 describes the essential features of the modelling process. The two major data inputs are network descriptions of the public and private transport modes and planning data; these describe the socio-economic

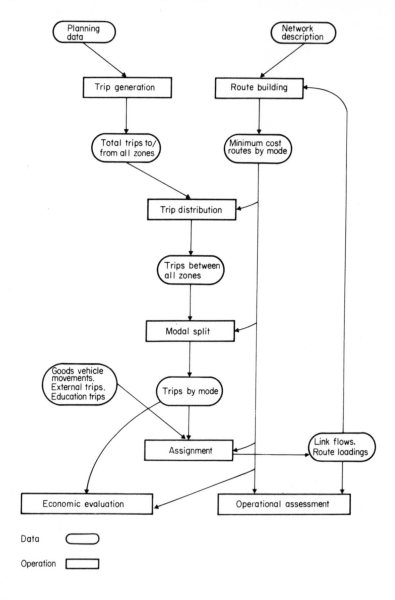

Fig. 7.1   Broad outline of modelling process

106

features relevant to transport movement.

Coventry and the surrounding district is divided into 158 geographical areas called 'zones'. For each zone, forecasts are made of the level of employment, the number of households (and their average income), and various services (shops, entertainment, educational facilities) in 1981. Using this data together with the average household income and car ownership in each zone, a forecast is derived for the number of trips generated by and attracted to each zone in the evening peak (here defined as the period 1530–1800 hours).

All 158 zones are connected by a road network and a public transport network. The road network is described as comprising nodes (or junctions) and links (or stretches of road), which join the various nodes and implicitly all the zones; each link is described in terms of its length and a speed–flow curve, which relates the speed of traffic on the link to the quantity of traffic using that link. A similar method is used to describe the public transport network, in which links include not only roads, but also routes used exclusively by public transport – e.g. railway tracks. In addition, however, public transport *lines,* which correspond to the services provided by public transport operators, are defined. Any transfer between lines involves a cost to the passenger.

Using these two network definitions, the cost of movement from all zones to all other zones can be calculated. Cost is defined as the weighted sum of the following four components:

(1) money cost (fares, petrol, parking charges, etc.);
(2) time spent in vehicle;
(3) time spent waiting for a vehicle (public transport only);
(4) time spent walking.

The trip-distribution model allocates trips from zone i to zone j as a function of the number of trip generations in zone i, the number of trip attractions in zone j, and the weighted cost – often called generalised cost – between zone i and j. The critical assumption is that the number of trips between two zones is a decreasing function of the cost of moving between the two zones, and for this study a negative exponential function was adopted. The mathematical form of the equation is[4]

$$T_{ij} = a_i \, b_j \, O_i \, D_j \exp(-\lambda C_{ij})$$

where T_{ij} = trips between i and j;
O_i = number of trip origins in zone i;
D_j = number of trip destinations in zone j;
C_{ij} = generalised cost of movement between i and j;

$a_i b_j$ are balancing factors; and
λ is a parameter.

Having obtained a matrix of movement between all zones, the modal-split sub-model divides travellers between the road network and the public transport system. Travellers without access to a car are assumed to use public transport. A rational individual with a car at his disposal chooses the mode that appears to him to have the minimum cost. In the case of a group of travellers with different valuations of the cost factors and different individual circumstances, it was assumed that the proportion using public transport is a function of the ratio of the costs of the two modes. Explicitly,

$$\frac{T_{ij}^{\;1}}{T_{ij}^{\;2}} = \exp\left(\beta\left(C_{ij}^{\;2} - C_{ij}^{\;1}\right)\right)$$

where $T_{ij}^{\;n}$ = trips by mode n between zone i and zone j;

$C_{ij}^{\;n}$ = generalised cost by mode n between zone i and zone j; and
β is a parameter.

Having determined the number of trips made by private and public transport between all zones, these trips are then assigned to their respective networks, assuming travellers use the shortest route. This gives the number of passengers on each public transport line and the number of vehicles on each link in the road network.

A number of iterations through these four stages of generation, distribution, modal split, and assignment are normally required, in order to ensure that a number of relationships are satisfied. In particular, it is necessary to ensure that the speed of traffic on each link of the road network bears the proper relationship to the amount of traffic using that link. This is referred to as 'capacity restraint'.

The main outputs of the model are the cost and amount of movement (in terms of trips) between all zones in the area, and the level of use of the two networks — road and public transport.

There is an intimate relationship between the model outlined above and the design of an automated transport service for a given route. The level of service offered on the route determines, in part, the level of passenger demand on the route; and the level and structure of passenger demand in turn affects the service that is provided. Fig. 7.2 describes in simplified form the relationship between the passenger demand produced by the transportation model, and the factors (walking time, waiting time, in-vehicle time, and fare) that are incorporated in the model as parameters of the new mode.

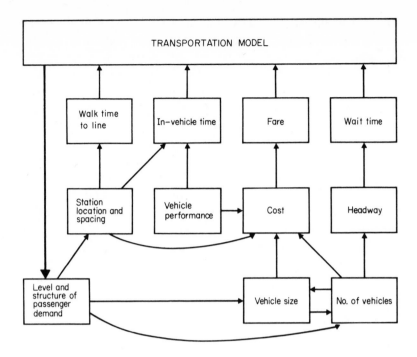

Fig. 7.2   The relationship between the transportation model and system design

Ideally, we wish to find an optimum solution that balances all the different factors affecting the level of service on the line and the cost of providing that service. The solution will necessarily have to rely on iterative methods in which trial values of the variables are inserted, and the outputs of the model compared for consistency and optimality. Later sections demonstrate some of these principles, although the details of the iterations that led up to the solution are omitted.

Passengers and a new mode

It might be objected that, since the model outlined above has been developed to simulate conventional modes of transport, it cannot be used to forecast passenger reaction to a new, and as yet unknown, mode. The critical assumption under attack is the claim that the attractiveness of a mode for a particular journey can be adequately described by a scalar quantity that is the weighted sum of a number of attributes, of which, in this instance, four are quantified and used. Even with existing modes, a perfect model would require us to consider many more than the time and cost variables listed above. The group of attributes contained in the phrase 'comfort and convenience' might be of particular relevance — this includes, among other things, seat dimensions, temperature, degree of weather protection, disturbance during a journey, and crowding. Research has so far failed to elicit acceptable estimates of passengers' valuations of these attributes. The question relevant in this context is whether the new mode (in this case, autotram) introduces new attributes perceptible to the potential passenger and likely significantly to affect both his valuation of the new mode and his subsequent reaction to it. On balance, it was felt that autotram did not differ from conventional modes in any way important enough significantly to affect its attractiveness (though the word 'significantly' should be interpreted in relation to the errors inherent in any attempt to forecast the future demand for transport).

The route study

The choice of which corridors in Coventry should be considered as potential routes for autotram was dictated by two considerations: first, we wished to examine routes that might be considered by a local authority wishing to make an important contribution to the solution of the city's transport problem, and that would give, in the broadest sense of the phrase, 'value for money'; secondly, we wished to examine routes with different demand patterns and in different urban settings in order to make it possible to reach general conclusions about the worth of autotram in different situations. Fortunately, the two requirements were found to coincide in the routes chosen for study.

The three radial routes (see Fig. 8.9) serve corridors of high passenger demand. No circumferential routes were chosen, as they failed to generate high levels of passenger demand; and, to anticipate a later conclusion, these will be required if a route is to prove an economic success. A radial route to the south of the city failed to generate sufficient demand and was not examined in detail. The western route followed joins the city centre to the railway station and then follows the main railway line (London–Coventry–Birmingham) through mixed residential and industrial districts. It can be at ground level for much of its length. The eastern corridor mostly passes through densely populated residential districts and for the main part needs to employ overhead track. The northern corridor connects Coventry with the two towns of Bedworth and Nuneaton. A railway line exists, but its failure to pass near to the city centre has prevented it from playing an important rôle in the movement of passengers. The autotram route uses the line of the railway up to a point about 4km from the city centre, after which it passes through residential and industrial districts and the main bus station before reaching the city centre. The total length of the three routes is 27·7km, representing 55·4km of single track.

The total capital cost of the system was estimated to be £24·3 million at 1973 prices. Running costs were estimated at £6·3 million per annum. Table 7.2 gives details.

Table 7.2

Costs of the autotram route in Coventry

	£'000 (1973 prices)	Cost per passenger km (p)
Capital costs		
Track (excluding control system)	17,900	1·00
Stations	1,250	·07
Control (track/central)	4,150	·23
Storage/maintenance areas	1,000	·06
Total	24,300	1·36

24,300 is equivalent to 2,676 per annum discounted at 10 per cent over 25 years

Running costs per annum		
Maintenance of track	220	·11
Maintenance and running of stations	378	·19
Maintenance and operation of non-vehicle control system	200	·10
Central management	50	·03
Vehicles: initial cost	1,086	·55
power	633	·32
maintenance (mechanical/electrical)	790	·40
maintenance (control system)	316	·16
Total	3,673	1·86
Total cost per annum, capital and running	6,349	3·22

Track

It was assumed that vehicles used rubber tyres for support, and track sidewalls for guidance and switching. Details of track costs for bottom-supported vehicles with sidewalls are given in Chapter 4. The low cost of ground-level track encourages its use wherever possible, and for over 50 per cent of the route in Coventry this was found feasible, especially where the track was near or adjacent to existing railway tracks. Elsewhere, overhead track was employed where ground-level track would have necessitated the closure of main roads or seriously restricted access to property. In the city centre, however, a short stretch of track was assumed to be underground. This was because it passed through areas where it was judged an overhead structure would be unacceptable on environmental grounds (this does not mean that overhead track was necessarily acceptable elsewhere — see Chapter 8). Table 7.3 gives the breakdown of cost.

Table 7.3

Track costs of the autotram route in Coventry

	Length (km)	Cost (£/m)	Total cost (£'000)
Ground level	36·4	204*	7,426
Overhead	15·8	523	8,263
Underground	3·2	690	2,208
Total	55·4	323	17,897

* This figure is higher than that given in Chapter 4 due to the need to construct overbridges, underpasses and retaining walls at certain points along the route.

Stations

The average cost of the 24 stations in the network is £52,000. This figure hides a wide variation in costs, since stations range from simple island stations catering for light passenger demand, to the underground city-centre station catering for the heavy passenger movements on the three radial routes. Average station spacing *within the city boundary* is just over 700 metres, which is somewhat greater than that found on tram or bus lines in most European towns and cities.

Although the exact locations of stations depend on such factors as where the route intersects with important roads or passes a group of commercial premises, some general idea of average spacing can be gleaned from examining the objectives involved. Essentially, the choice of where to locate a station is an attempt to balance the competing demands for, on the one hand, a short walk to a station, and, on the other, low cost and a short journey time. If the distance between stations is short, so will walks be, but the financial costs of stations for the route will be high and in-vehicle journey times will be long.

A model outlined by Black[5] was used to estimate the optimum station spacing under different assumptions. The variables and parameters used in the model are given below.

		Value that favours close station spacing	Values examined
Passenger:			
average walk speed	w	low	5 km/hour
average journey length	d	low	5.6 km
value of time in vehicle	t_i	low	30 pence/hour
value of time walking	t_w	high	60 pence/hour
density	p	high	50–250 passengers/km/hour
Vehicle:			
rate of acceleration/ deceleration	q	high	1·5 m/s²
cruise speed	v	low	48 km/hour
stop time in station	b	low	10–20s
cost (time-related only)	c_v	low	0–10 pence/hour/seat
load factor	l	high	0·33
Station:			
cost	c_s	low	0–500 pence/hour

The objective function (which is minimised) is the average total cost of passenger movement, which is defined in this context as walking time plus in-vehicle time plus vehicle and station cost:

$$t_w \cdot \frac{1}{2\,s\cdot w} + t_i \cdot \frac{d}{v_a} + c_v \cdot \frac{d}{l \cdot v_a} + c_s \cdot \frac{s}{p}$$

where s is the number of stations per km and v_a is the average vehicle speed as a function of s, a, v and b.

113

The results strongly suggest that, with the parameter values shown here, station spacing on an autotram route should be over 500m and, with the particular assumptions relevant to Coventry, about 700m. This implies average walking times higher than those that would be expected with existing public transport. It might be argued that the results of the analysis are unacceptable, and that any new mode should provide a service at least as good in all its attributes as the one it is replacing. This seems to be an excessively restrictive criterion. It would be surprising if any new technology led to a product superior in all aspects to the one it is partially or completely replacing. Aircraft have almost entirely replaced ocean liners on Atlantic journeys, yet many aspects of aircraft operation (space per passenger, for example) are inferior to their liner equivalents. Modes of transport must be judged on their overall attractiveness rather than particular components.

Two arguments that could be advanced for smaller station spacing than that derived from the above model are that the cost or inconvenience of walking increases more than linearly with distance, or that considerations of equity require that no household in an urban area should be more than x km from a station on the public transport network.

Control

The vehicles are assumed to operate within a simple fixed-block control system that allows headways as low as 24 seconds. A central computer supervises all traffic movements, issues speed commands, and controls switching and despatching. Vehicle computers control speed, acceleration, position, and door operation. The estimate of £75,000 per km for control equipment on the track and at central control (i.e. excluding vehicles) is based on cost figures for the Airtrans system at Dallas/Fort Worth airport and estimates for the installation of VAL in Lille.[6] Published cost figures given for the Morgantown control system suggest a higher figure (£150,000 per km), but this refers to a more sophisticated control system.

Running costs

Maintenance costs of track are based on estimates made for the Tracked Hovercraft track. Almost half the costs are due to maintenance of power-collection equipment rather than the structure itself. The operating cost of stations is equivalent to an average of just over £15,000 per annum. The larger stations are manned throughout the day. Maintenance of lifts, ticket machinery, automatic entrance and exit gates, surveillance of unmanned stations by closed-circuit television, cleaning, lighting, and so on, all contribute to the cost figure.

Operation of the control system handling, variations in the number of vehicles in service, reacting to emergencies and maintaining control equipment amounts to £200,000 per annum. Central management services are estimated to be in the region of £50,000 per annum.

Vehicles

For this study, cost estimates refer to a vehicle with a carrying capacity of 40 passengers (see below for a justification of this size). A vehicle comprises two equal-size cars powered by rotary electric motors and running on rubber tyres. The size of each car is 2m by 4·5m, giving an average area per passenger of 0·45m^2 − quite generous by public transport standards. Total capital cost of each vehicle is £28,500 (or £4,688 per annum with a life of 10 years).

Maintenance of vehicles needs to be to a high standard. Vehicle failures that bring the vehicle to a halt cause serious disruption to the service, and heavy maintenance expenditure is required to prevent this from happening too regularly. Maintenance of one of the cars on the Victoria Line (only half of which are powered) is 2·7p per km (1973 prices), and for a London Transport bus the figure is 4·0p per km. Although the autotram cars are smaller, requiring less cleaning, the number of components requiring checking and occasional replacement is similar. We estimate maintenance costs at 2·5p per km. Maintenance of vehicle control equipment is estimated at 1·0p per km. Overall operating costs are 23·2p per vehicle km, compared with a capital-cost equivalent of 17·0p per vehicle km − a total of 40·2p per vehicle km.

Costs and uncertainty

Considerable uncertainty is attached to cost estimates of proposed transport installations, and when this installation incorporates new and unproven technology the margin of uncertainty is substantially enhanced. The estimate of 40·2p per vehicle km for a 40-place vehicle represents a 'best' estimate and should be considered as the centre of a range. It neither assumes a major technological breakthrough − in the type of structural materials used or in control techniques, for instance − nor includes any contribution for research and development costs; for this reason, it does not bear close comparison with the cost estimates that have been published for the Morgantown system. It is also assumed that the structures and vehicles are produced in sufficient quantity to allow the economies of long production runs.

Service and demand

In any transport system there is an intimate relationship between service, demand and cost. In a reserved-track system with a capital cost independent (or almost independent) of demand, cost per passenger km is low when demand is high. Similarly, if the vehicle size and occupancy are constant, waiting time will be reduced and hence service improved when demand is high. The service provided on the Coventry routes during the peak period is a function of four factors:

- fare = 2p + 1·6 p/km. It is assumed the fare covers operating cost only and makes no (significant) contribution to capital costs. The fare level is the same as that assumed for bus operation in 1981. A justification for this policy is given later.
- average journey speed. This is a function of average cruise speed, rate of acceleration/deceleration, and vehicle stop time in stations. It varies for different journeys on the route. The average journey speed for trips during the peak period within Coventry is approximately 35km/h, which corresponds to a cruise speed of 48km/h; acceleration/deceleration rates of 1·5m/s; a stop time in stations of 15 seconds; and station spacing of 700m. Speeds may be slightly faster in the peak period with shorter station stop times.
- average waiting times. Average vehicle headways are about 40 seconds in the peak, and 76 seconds in the off-peak period. Average waiting times should be below 30 seconds throughout the peak period and less than 1 minute in off-peak periods.
- average walk times. This varies over the route from a minimum of less than 300m in the centre to over 500m on the outskirts. Individual passengers may walk up to twice these distances.

Passenger demand

The estimates of fare and service level inserted into the transportation model allow us to estimate demand during a typical evening peak period (1530–1800 hours) in 1981. Statistics from the Coventry Transportation Study were used to estimate all-day and weekend demand. Table 7.4 gives a summary of passenger demand and vehicle requirements, Fig. 7.3 gives details of passenger loadings on the routes, and Fig. 7.4 gives details of passengers boarding and alighting at individual stations.

116

Table 7.4

Summary of passenger demand on Coventry routes

	Peak	Off-peak	Total (or average)
Weekday operation			
Duration (hours)	5	11	16
Passenger flow (passenger km)	406,915	282,771	689,686
Passenger flow per hour (passenger km/hour)	81,383	25,706	43,105
Load factor	0·4	0·25	0·3
Vehicle flow (vehicle km)	25,430	28,281	53,711
Vehicle flow (vehicle km/hour)	5,086	2,571	3,356
Average headway (seconds)	40	76	
Average vehicle km per day	95	105	200
Annual			
Passenger flow (million passenger km)	103·7	93·3	197·0
Passengers (5·6 km per trip), millions			35·2
Vehicle flow (million vehicle km)	6·5	9·3	15·8
Average distance per vehicle (km)			68,398

Route length = 55·4 km
Average journey speed = 35 km per hour
Vehicle size = 40 places
Number of vehicles = 231 (10 per cent spare)

Vehicle size

The choice of vehicle size is determined by a number of factors. The main arguments in favour of small vehicles rest on their ability to

— give short passenger waiting times,
— use light, cheap and less intrusive guideways, and
— allow small, cheap and less intrusive stations (as a result of short platforms and small waiting areas).

On the other hand, large vehicles mean

— lower vehicle costs per passenger, and

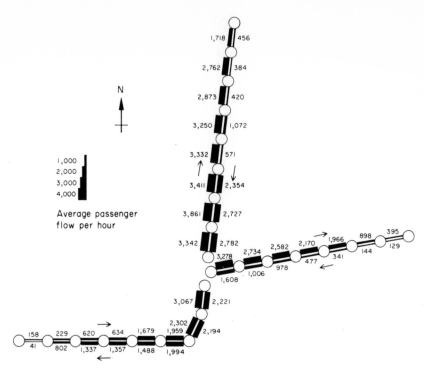

Route	North	West	East	All
Mean flow	1,642	1,168	1,289	1,469
Mean outward flow	2,553	1,224	1,929	
Mean inward flow	731	1,112	649	
Maximum link flow	3,861	3,067	3,278	3,861
Ratio outward/inward flow	3·5	1·1	3·0	
Ratio: $\dfrac{\text{maximum link flow}}{\text{mean flow}}$	2·4	2·6	2·5	2·6

Fig. 7.3   Passenger flows on the network, evening peak 1981

— low costs of control for a given capacity (or a higher capacity for a given total control cost).

It is not clear whether, on comfort grounds, passengers prefer smaller or larger vehicles (in the six- to 50-place range).

The process of choosing the size of vehicle to be used can be viewed as an optimisation problem, with minimum cost (money cost plus time costs of passengers) as the objective function, and with passenger-comfort criterion and cost functions as constraints in the model. The control

118

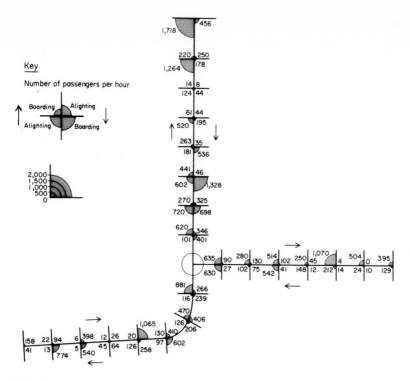

Fig. 7.4   Passenger flows through stations, evening peak 1981

system can be viewed either as part of the optimisation problem or as an external constraint. In practice the problem is rather difficult to define with any confidence. In particular, there is no reliable method for valuing small differences in waiting times. Similarly, cost functions for track, stations and vehicles as a function of vehicle size are not easy to construct. For these reasons we have defined the problem as one of finding a small vehicle size (and hence short waiting times) that is compatible with providing the necessary capacity on the system and that does not involve off-line stations.

The demand for places on the Coventry system varies both spatially and temporally. Regular peaks will occur at certain places on the system and at certain times of the day. Occasionally, circumstances will create very high levels of demand over a short period (demand following a football match provides a classic example). We define the maximum demand the system should be able to meet as the average demand in the peak half-hour at the peak load point on an average weekday — the temporal and spatial peak. If this peak is exceptionally severe compared with the

119

next highest peak figure, there may be some justification for attempting to reduce it by suitable pricing policies or by failing to provide adequate capacity — resulting in queueing or in lost passengers. The latter method might be used when the operator feels that the extra cost of meeting the demand is too high, and thus allows the quality of service to fall. In a sense, the acceptance of standing passengers is another example of the cost of maintaining certain standards ('seats for all') being considered too high. The peak link demand found in Coventry was 3,861 passengers per hour in the evening peak. Evidence from surveys of public transport in Coventry suggest that the flow in the peak half-hour is likely to be in the region of 1·5 times the average flow in the 2½-hour period from 1530—1600 hours (both defined in units of 'per hour'). The peak spatial and temporal demand is therefore 5,790 passengers per hour.

The combinations of vehicle size and headway that can meet a specified passenger demand is given by the identity: capacity per hour = maximum passenger flow per hour = vehicle size (places) x 3600/minimum headway (seconds). Thus, a vehicle with 40 places and a minimum headway of 24 seconds gives a theoretical capacity of 6,000 passengers per hour — just above our requirements.

For a number of reasons this simple calculation should be treated with caution. It is unlikely that the minimum headway of 24 seconds could be maintained for any substantial period of time. Delays to vehicles in stations are bound to occur, especially during the peak period and with nearly full vehicles. It is not possible to estimate accurately the importance of these delays, but it seems likely that a shortfall in capacity of as much as 10 per cent might occur. This can be counteracted by various measures, all of which attempt to ensure that vehicles are not delayed in stations longer than necessary. The methods used include warning lights and bells before the doors close, and preventing passengers from entering the platform area just before the vehicle is due to leave the station.

The assumption of a vehicle able to carry a maximum of 40 passengers must also be viewed as an approximation. The vehicles allow an average floor area per passenger of 0.45m^2, but if we accept the London Transport figures for vehicle capacity,[7] the autotram vehicles could carry up to 80 people. It should be pointed out that if this does happen (and it is difficult to stop it happening at least occasionally), then the vehicles must be designed to cater for the extra weight. Thus we can see that, if passengers are willing to accept some degree of discomfort, a capacity of at least 6,000 passengers per hour can be maintained even when headway falls below 24 seconds. This flexibility in the definition of passenger-

120

carrying capacity may prove to be important if the forecasts of passenger demand are found to be too low.

The average load factor of vehicles (i.e. the number of passengers divided by the number of places) falls below 1·0 for a number of reasons. Demand along a route varies and, even though the load factor is 1·0 on the peak link, the average load factor for the route as a whole tends to be about 0·4 for a radial route in urban areas (see Fig. 7.2 for the ratio of average passenger flow to maximum link flow in the three Coventry corridors). Operators may be prepared to accept even lower load factors if low waiting times are important (and if the size of vehicles cannot be changed). For this reason we adopted a figure of 0·25 during the off-peak period, although on strictly economic grounds — comparing the extra cost with the reduction in waiting times — the improvement in service is probably not justified.

Design of services

To meet the forecast passenger demand in Coventry at least four service patterns are possible (see Fig. 7.5). Type (a) is a simple corridor service. On journeys through the city centre passengers change vehicles, but, if the city centre station is designed carefully, the walk should be short — perhaps a few metres across a platform. Type (b) avoids the low load factors found at the suburban end of corridors; this reduces operating costs but makes it necessary for some passengers to change vehicles or wait for one going to their destination in the outskirts. Extra lengths of track, together with switches, are needed at short-turn points. Type (c) reduces the proportion of passengers who need to change at the centre. Its main disadvantage occurs when the three corridors have different levels of demand: load factors would be low on corridors where demand is low. Slightly more flexible is type (d), which connects two corridors. This makes it possible for passengers to make any journey without changing but it does require some passengers to wait for the correct vehicle for their journey. It may also suffer from the disadvantage of (c) in being unable to cater efficiently for different levels of demand on the three corridors.

As the number of corridors served by the system increases, types (c) and (d) will not be justified. Type (c) would rarely avoid the need for changing vehicles at the centre, and with type (d) passengers would have to spend too much time waiting for the correct vehicle, merely to avoid, at a maximum, one change.

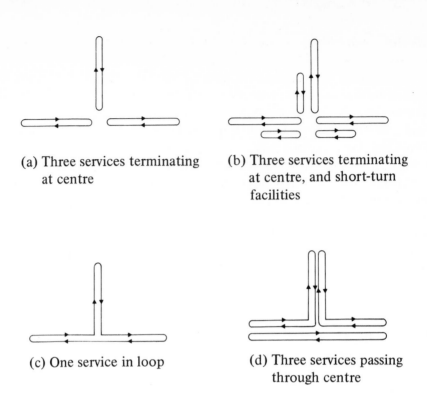

(a) Three services terminating at centre

(b) Three services terminating at centre, and short-turn facilities

(c) One service in loop

(d) Three services passing through centre

Fig. 7.5   Possible design of services in Coventry

Cost-benefit appraisal

This section considers the costs and benefits resulting from the installation of autotram in Coventry. An important objective of cost-benefit analysis is to value the effects of a change in terms of a common unit. In practice this is always money, and if the change refers to the output of commodities sold and purchased in the market place this poses no great difficulty. However, in transport, one commodity that is not sold and purchased directly in the market is time, and in recent years considerable effort has been directed to estimating the value passengers attach to changes in travelling time, whether this be time spent in a vehicle or time spent walking or waiting. Most of the research suggests that the value people attach to a saving in travelling time is about one-quarter their wage or salary rate. Although a range of uncertainty is attached to this figure, research findings have been surprisingly consistent over time and over

122

different continents – at least in advanced Western societies.[8] The research has also shown that the value attached to savings in time spent waiting and walking is about twice that attached to in-vehicle time, presumably a reflection of the difference in comfort of the two circumstances.

As a matter of UK government policy, it has been decided that economic evaluations dealing with the value of time should use an 'equity' value based on the level of average earnings in the country. Use of a value of time correlated with income would, it is felt, provide a bias favouring investment projects in rich areas and the better-off groups in society.

A number of other assumptions are made concerning the value of time. It is assumed that the value increases over time at the same rate as the increase in real incomes. Different values are used for travel in the course of work (time saved is valued at the average wage rate, to represent the opportunity cost of the output foregone) and for travel by children either accompanied by adults or to and from places of education.

The 'equity' value of time for leisure travel or commuting in 1981 is 28 pence per hour (valued in terms of prices prevailing in 1973).

Costs

The usual method of structuring the cost-benefit appraisal when dealing with investment projects is to compare the cost of the investment with net benefits – i.e. benefits minus costs (which usually include running costs) – resulting from the investment. The net-benefit figure takes into account all recurrent expenditure (such as changes in operating costs) and changes in benefits to users of, and to any other parties that might be affected either directly or indirectly by, the investment project. Under this definition, the total cost of the automated system in Coventry is £24·3 million (1973 prices).

The model results together with some other adjustments lead to an estimate of the net benefits resulting from investment in the year 1981. The ratio of net benefits to investment cost in its first year of introduction is known as the first-year rate of return. A better appreciation of the worth of the investment is gained by considering the flow of benefits over the entire life of the investment. If this is to be done, the principle of discounting has to be introduced. The essential idea of discounting is contained in the phrase 'better jam today than jam tomorrow': individuals tend to prefer more immediate benefits to the promise of benefits later. Two reasons are advanced to justify the existence of a 'time-discount' factor. First, people are likely to enjoy a higher real income in the future (this applies to the community as a whole, although the prospects for individuals within it may vary), and hence the intensity of their wants or needs will no doubt reduce as incomes increase. Secondly, individuals tend to underestimate future benefits when there is a possibility of death intervening, although there is little doubt that this tendency is reinforced by a common human failure to resist the attraction of present needs. The rate of time discount recommended for use in cost-benefit studies in the UK, to represent society's preference for earlier benefits, is 10 per cent per annum.

Another important concept associated with flows of costs and benefits over time is the internal rate of return. This is the rate of time discount that equates all benefits, whenever they occur, to the cost of the investment. Formally, it is the value of r that satisfies the equation

$$\sum_{t=-\infty}^{t=\infty} \frac{NB_t - I_t}{(1+r)^t} = 0$$

where I = investment cost, and
NB = net benefits.

If r is greater than 10 per cent, this implies that the (discounted) sum of net benefits is greater than the value of the investment. Hence, there is a *prima facie* case that the investment yields a surplus of benefit over cost given society's rate of time discount (which we assume to be 10 per cent).

Benefits

It was assumed earlier that fares on the automated system in Coventry in 1981 will be the same as those on the bus system. With the introduction of the new system, some public transport passengers who previously used a bus for certain journeys will find that, for the same money expenditure, they can now use a faster service involving less waiting time (although, perhaps, a slightly greater walking time). As a result they will be better off, owing to the time they save, and may even decide to make slightly different journeys and perhaps even change their place of employment. Some people who previously used private transport may find the new public transport sufficiently attractive to persuade them to use it instead. In consequence, the remaining road users will also benefit, since they will find the roads less congested. The simulation suggests that trips by public transport will increase by 9·3 per cent as a result of the introduction of the new system. Table 7.5 gives a summary of the benefits.

124

Table 7.5

Summary of cost-benefit appraisal, 1981 (£'000, 1973 prices)

	Peak	Off-peak	Total
Investment cost			*24,300*
Benefits			
USER BENEFITS			
Public transport users	865	783	1,648
Private transport users	86	65	151
Freight transport	17	86	103
Total	968	934	1,902
OTHER ADJUSTMENTS			
Public transport operating surplus	29	27	56
Gap between road users, perceived and actual costs	111	50	161
Absence of buses from highway	126	10	136
Total	266	87	353
TOTAL BENEFITS			*2,255*
First-year rate of return (per cent)			*9·3*

The user benefits represent the sum of two elements. First, they represent the savings in money and cost accruing to travellers due to the introduction of the new mode, assuming their trip pattern remains constant. But in practice this will rarely happen: the new, more attractive service will persuade them to travel to different destinations. Their expenditure (time plus money) may then actually increase, but this could hardly be conceived of as a disbenefit.

If a person travels to zone x before the investment and zone y after, we need to know four costs before we can estimate the net benefit (or disbenefit) from the change. If the costs are $c(x)$, $c(y)$ before, and $c^1(x)$,

$c^1(y)$ after the investment, we can say the increase in benefit that the person derives from going to y instead of x is (a) not greater than $c(y) - c(x)$, or he would have gone to y in the 'before' situation, and (b) not less than $c^1(y) - c^1(x)$, or he would go to x in the 'after' situation. Without further information, we assume that the benefit of going to y rather than x lies halfway between the maximum and minimum figure, i.e.

$$\tfrac{1}{2} \left[c(y) - c(x) + c^1(y) - c^1(x) \right]$$

This argument can be extended[9] to derive a formula for estimating total user benefits, viz.

$$\tfrac{1}{2} \sum_{ij} (T_{ij} + T_{ij}^1)(C_{ij} - C_{ij}^1)$$

where T_{ij}, T_{ij}^1 = trips between i and j before and after the change, and
C_{ij}, C_{ij}^1 = cost of movement between i and j before and after a change.

Using this formula, we find the user benefits accruing to different groups of travellers. As expected, the group of transport users to benefit most from the new installation are existing public transport users and those attracted to the new mode from private transport. Over 85 per cent of user benefits are enjoyed by this group, but significant benefits also flow to other groups. About 50 per cent of all user benefits occur in the peak hours.

A number of adjustments need to be made to the total user benefits. Although the automated public transport system yields a small surplus of revenue over operating costs, the situation in bus operation is somewhat different. This is associated with the co-ordination of services on the two public transport modes. It is assumed that the introduction of a new reserved-track service along a corridor will result in most of the original bus services along that route being withdrawn. Some, however, will remain, especially those that follow the line of the automated system for only part of its route. The choice facing the operator lies between two extremes: either the service is cut to maintain revenue per vehicle km run; or, if this proves difficult (because the spatial peak in demand on a route occurs at a point that is not near the new system, or because the drop in the quality of service is felt to be too severe), the deficit on that route increases (or surplus falls). The use of buses as feeder services to the new transport mode may also prove to be not very profitable to the bus operator. All in all, the introduction of the new automated mode is likely to prove very traumatic to the bus operator, and careful forward planning, both of overall public transport operation and the institutional framework in which it operates, is needed.

The second adjustment takes account of the tendency for car owners to underestimate the real cost of using their cars. Numerous surveys have suggested that car users assume that the cost of using a car for an extra journey is no more than the cost of petrol and oil. These may be the only costs the user anticipates at the decision-making time, but a journey means that other costs are incurred as well. Most components (tyres provide a prime example) depreciate — or wear out — as a function of distance run. As maintenance costs in the form of replacement of components or a regular service take the form of intermittent costs, most motorists tend to ignore them in calculating the cost of an extra or marginal journey. Similarly, insurance costs are usually paid annually (for administrative reasons), even though the risk of an accident in any time-period almost certainly increases as a linear function of distance run. Accidents also impose costs other than those borne by the motorist: these take the form of traffic disruption and hospital costs. It is estimated that the difference between the costs assumed by a car owner and the resources he consumes on a journey is 0·9p per km, which also takes into account the non-resource or tax element in the price of petrol.

Automated systems using reserved tracks have high track costs. Although the track costs of bus operation are not usually estimated in any accounting or cost-benefit framework, they are just as real as those on an automated system. They include: (a) that part of road maintenance and traffic management attributable to bus operation; and (b) use of scarce roadspace, which interferes with other traffic movement. The first is likely to be small — almost certainly less than 1p per vehicle km; but the second is more significant. The withdrawal of bus services along a corridor means a higher average speed for other vehicles and hence time savings for these users. (There is a possibility, though not a serious one, that the introduction of an automated system may lead to an increase in car use, due to the increase in the attractiveness of roads as buses are withdrawn being greater than that of the new public transport system!) An estimate of savings to road users as a result of the withdrawal of buses depends largely on the level of congestion on the road system (the higher the level of congestion, the greater the benefit of withdrawing the marginal vehicle). Table 7.5 gives estimates for the effect of these two factors in Coventry.

The rate of return

These calculations showed the first-year rate of return to be 9·3 per cent.

127

The internal rate of return depends critically on the rate of growth of passenger demand on the network. If the value of time grows at 3 per cent per year, in line with real income (and official recommendations), and if passenger demand remains stable for the life of the track structure (25 years), the internal rate of return (IRR) would be just under 10 per cent. If demand grows by 3 per cent per year, the IRR would be nearly 13 per cent. [10]

Investment projects in the public sector are expected to yield a rate of return of at least 10 per cent. The system in Coventry thus seems to be on the margin of acceptability. But when we compare the expected rate of return on investment to the rates for other transport schemes examined by the Coventry Transportation Study, we find that from an economic viewpoint the system represents a relatively poor use of investment funds. For instance, the three road schemes examined yielded first-year rates of return of 23, 26·9 and 13·9 per cent respectively — figures that are by no means unusual for road investment in medium-sized towns like Coventry. Thus, on strictly economic criteria, the automated system does not present a very attractive use of resources compared to other potential applications.

Fare levels

It was assumed that the fare levels on the automated system would be the same as those prevailing on the bus system in 1981. This would mean that revenue would cover operating costs but not the interest payments or repayments on the capital borrowed. If we follow the economist's principle that price should equal marginal cost or, in everyday terms, that a passenger should not be charged a fare in excess of the extra cost he imposes on the operator and other travellers, then there seems a strong case for a fare policy aimed at covering only operating costs, which for practical purposes can be assumed to be marginal costs.

A further argument for such a policy is that it would be desirable to maintain comparability with the pricing methods currently used on the road system, where no direct charges are imposed for use of the capital equipment. A policy of covering operating costs also provides a clear management objective, unlike a zero-fares policy. This objection to zero fares can be overcome, but perhaps a more serious objection to them in the case of a limited reserved-track system is that the subsidy would be biased in favour of a limited number of people living near the routes, while a large number of people would be forced to contribute to a subsidy. Zero fares would need to be justified in the context of an overall policy towards transport, and public transport in particular.

If the equipment for automated ticket collection and checking is expensive to install and maintain, then zero fares have an added attraction. But some simplification might be achieved by the use of a flat-fares policy. For instance, the Coventry study showed that a 10p fare would generate a level of passenger demand and revenue similar to that derived from the conventional pricing policy of charging per kilometre. The structure of passenger demand would be different, but total passenger kilometres would not be radically changed.

Other matters

The previous sections have described a formal assessment of an automated system in Coventry. One possible criticism of it is that the formal nature of the assessment framework fails to take account of certain effects (especially those that cannot be quantified) and takes insufficient account of the uncertainties necessarily contained within an appraisal of new technology, many of the effects of which lie far into the future. Both these arguments have some strength, but the great difficulty is to estimate the relative importance of the effects to which they refer (environmental problems are left to the next chapter).

A frequently canvassed advantage of automated systems, and one that might improve their position in the cost-benefit framework, is the improvement in 'comfort and convenience' offered — that is, in addition to reduced travelling and waiting times. Covered or completely enclosed stations are the rule, and vehicles are often air-conditioned and fitted with seats of similar standard to those in first-class railway carriages. These and similar embellishments are invariably included by developers to emphasise the advantages of the new mode over the conventional modes. However, the critical question is whether automated systems have an inherent advantage over other forms of transport — whether there is anything in the concept that means it is easier or cheaper to provide a higher standard of comfort and convenience. In the area of ride quality, automated systems do seem to have an advantage over road-based public transport. The smooth track, carefully designed horizontal and lateral acceleration/ deceleration profiles, together with the absence of the stop—go movement characteristic of buses, should guarantee a high standard of ride comfort. On the other hand, some aspects of reserved-track operation may prove to be particularly inconvenient. For instance, a climb of 5m or more to a platform serving overhead track could prove a severe disincentive to many travellers — particularly the old and infirm and those with luggage or pushchairs. Lifts or escalators can be installed, but only at a heavy cost.

Uncertainty exists in all forecasts, and, when the forecast involves estimates of the cost and impact of new technology, the range of uncertainty is much increased. Looking back at these forecasts in 1981, it will doubtless be said that the costs were wrong; and, after some experience of a demonstration project, it will be found that passenger reaction to travelling was different from that outlined here. Only time and experience will reduce this uncertainty. Until then we can but say that the estimates are the best we can make with the present evidence. At the moment it seems that the economic benefit of an automated system in Coventry is in the balance, but if costs are found to be less than stated, or performance better, or passenger and non-passenger reaction more favourable than expected, then the prospects for a novel system become much brighter.

Notes

[1] *Coventry Transportation Study,* City of Coventry, 1972.

[2] Ibid., para. 37.01.

[3] Ibid., table 9.01.

[4] For the derivation of this equation, see A.G. Wilson, *Entropy in Urban and Regional Modelling,* Pion, 1972.

[5] I.G. Black, 'Optimisation and system parameters', in I.G. Black *et al., Advanced Transport Systems in British Cities. Symposium 73 Proceedings,* Warwick University, 1973.

[6] *Amélioration du plan de transports en commun création d'une première ligne du Métro, 1974.*

[7] S.A. Driver, 'Design of railway rolling stock for heavy urban services', Paper 10 in *Rapid Transit Vehicles for City Services,* Institution of Mechanical Engineers, 1971. See Chapter 5 for further details.

[8] A.J. Harrison and D.A. Quarmby, *The Value of Time in Transport Planning,* ECMT Symposium, 1969.

[9] H. Neuberger, 'User benefit in the evaluation of transport and land use', *Journal of Transport Economics and Policy,* January 1971.

[10] Strictly speaking, an accurate estimate of the IRR requires an estimate of the change in all variables (demand, cost, values, etc.) over time. For the computations in the text it was assumed that the construction period was three years and that net benefits grew at a rate of 3 per cent (or 6 per cent) for 25 years (the life of the investment).

8 Environment

The problem of harmonising forms of transport investment with an existing environment has a long history: as long ago as 1846, a House of Commons Select Committee vetoed a series of plans by which railway companies aimed to achieve extensive penetration of the City and West End areas of London, and in the mid-nineteenth century attempts to develop city centre terminals in other cities created a number of financial crises in railway companies, so great was the cost entailed in the disturbance to densely populated areas.[1]

Such problems continue to affect the development of any 'all or nothing' transport facility: a city may have considerable areas that can accommodate a length of motorway or a section of railway without offending anyone, but no one needs a motorway that links one bottleneck with another, or a railway that is environmentally acceptable because it fails to penetrate the major centres of activity.

The history of the street tramway has also been influenced by environmental objections. Overhead power lines (sometimes replaced by the more costly conduit system) and the noise generated by steel wheels limited the expansion of the tramway system in some cities and contributed to its demise.

A major plank in the argument put forward by proponents of autotram is the ease with which it can be introduced into existing cities.[2] Autotrams would be quiet, and could negotiate tight curves (down to a 10m radius). The system would thus be highly flexible and could be woven around the existing activities of an urban area, involving no extensive demolition; indeed, heavy emphasis has been placed upon the need for such systems to be attractive when built overhead, since it has been assumed that ground-level track would be too disruptive and underground track too expensive.

In this chapter we are as much concerned with the implications that environmental factors will have for the system design as with the effect of an actual system on the environment. When considering the effect of a system for which, in this country, a prototype does not exist, there is no reason to assume that the design is 'fixed', and we shall consider a range of possible designs of track, stations and vehicles.

The impact of track

Chapter 4 referred to three types of track — elevated, ground-level and underground. The cost associated with each type of construction can be conveniently divided into three components: construction cost, opportunity cost of land, and environmental cost.

Construction costs are dealt with in Chapter 4. By 'opportunity cost of land' we mean the cost of not using the land for other purposes. Environmental costs represent the deterioration in amenities suffered by people who are at any time in the vicinity of the track. Environmental effects that might be generated by autotram are: noise, visual intrusion, air pollution, vibration, dirt, changes in the amount of daylight and sunlight, and loss of privacy. Sometimes the effect is complicated by assumptions made about other factors: for instance, the net effect on noise and air pollution is influenced by the change in private vehicle use after the installation of autotram.

Table 8.1 ranks the different levels of cost for the three types of track. Underground track has the lowest opportunity and environmental cost but, on the other hand, the highest cost of construction. Elevated track is assumed to have the highest environmental cost. The visual intrusion, the change in the amount of daylight and sunlight, and the loss of privacy caused by an elevated track are all likely to be higher than with a track built at ground level. Ground-level track, however, has a high opportunity cost, although this does depend to a large extent on the exact location of the route. If, for instance, the land alongside an existing railway is used, then the alternative use for the land is limited and the cost low. Elsewhere — in the centre of a road, for instance — opportunity costs may be high, especially if the location of the track leads to a high degree of severance between neighbourhoods. It may be possible in some instances to reduce severance by using partially submerged ground-level track with frequent crossing points. The main disadvantage of this approach is that it tends to increase construction costs, especially where services need to be moved.

The following sections in this chapter examine in detail some of the environmental effects associated with elevated track — including noise, which is also associated with ground-level track. The problems posed by the opportunity cost of ground-level track are also considered before we turn to the special difficulties of introducing an autotram system into Coventry.

Fig. 8.1 distils the range of possible elevated-track designs into five basic types, representing different visual effects imposed on people adjacent or below the track. Track types I, II and III correspond to

Table 8.1

Rank order of three components of track cost

Type of construction	Type of cost		
	Construction	Opportunity	Environmental
Ground-level	3	1	2
Elevated	2	2	1
Underground	1	3	3

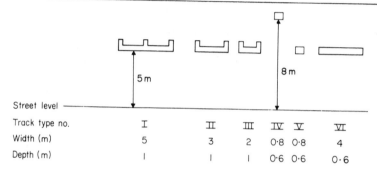

Fig. 8.1   Alternative designs of elevated track

bottom-supported vehicles with sidewall guidance. I is a double track and II and III are 'wide' and 'narrow' single tracks respectively. IV is a single track suitable for a suspended vehicle. Track type V is suitable for straddle-type vehicles. Type VI can refer to a double-track centre-guidance system or double-track straddle vehicles, although in the latter case there would be a gap in the centre of the track.

The problems of environmental assessment

The increase in the ownership and use of cars during the 1960s stimulated the search for appropriate techniques for assessing the economic consequences of alternative transport-investment strategies. At the same time, public awareness of the environmental consequences of transport investment stimulated attempts to develop techniques of environmental assessment that could be used in parallel with the techniques of economic assessment. A successful environmental appraisal involves relating an

133

objective (i.e. value-free) measure of a disturbing (or enjoyable) activity to people's welfare. For instance, numerous attempts have been made to relate an index of noise (based on sound pressure and frequency) to people's discomfort or displeasure. But, due to the complexity of people's reactions it has been found impossible to derive a well-defined measure of the change in welfare induced by a change in noise level. Two notable difficulties are the variability of human response to the same stimuli, and the need to distinguish between perceived and real welfare.

Where we possess some crude knowledge of people's discomfort, it may be possible to introduce 'standards' regulating the maximum level of disturbance permitted. For over a hundred years, the Public Health Acts in the UK have established standards of hygiene to govern the erection and maintenance of residential property. Other statutes define the tolerable limits of various forms of nuisance: where physical health is involved, standards are likely to be very strict (this would apply to fire regulations and the discharge of radioactive waste, for instance), but, where nuisance is all that is involved, they are likely to be drawn at a fairly generous point, and tend to define not so much where a nuisance becomes acceptable, but where it becomes intolerable for the vast majority of the population. Such standards are essentially safety nets rather than codes of good behaviour, and it seems fair to assume that, where the introduction of an autotram system violates an existing standard, then, irrespective of how it behaves with respect to other standards, it must be ruled unacceptable. The converse is, of course, not true: just because a system is held to be tolerable, this does not imply that it is acceptable.

It should, however, be appreciated that only certain kinds of disturbance may be analysed in this way. We are so ignorant of people's perception of some levels of environmental disturbance that we are unable to relate the disturbance to any scale. Aesthetic judgments are incapable of being related to any scale of measurement. It could not, for instance, be said that a large autotram track will in all cases be less attractive than a small one. This will depend upon its position, its relation to other buildings, and intimate details of its design. In these cases we are not only ignorant of the way people trade off different levels of benefit and disturbance, but we are also ignorant of the ordinal relationship between levels of disturbance and the physical properties of a particular development.

In the investigation of the impact of an autotram system, the standards used were: rights of open space, daylight, sunlight, and noise. Design guides with respect to the four objectives have been published, though only those referring to rights of open space and, to a limited extent, noise are embodied in statutory form.

134

Rights of open space

Rights of open space for residential building are defined under the 1965 building regulations. Every façade containing a window must possess a zone of open space in front of that façade, the depth of that zone being not less than 4m.[3]

Daylight

Daylight is conventionally measured in terms of 'daylight factors'. A 'daylight factor' is the percentage of daylight received at any point, to the daylight available from a completely unobstructed sky, i.e.

$$DF = \frac{E_1}{E_2} \times 100$$

where E_1 = daylight at the measuring point, and
E_2 = daylight available from the whole sky.

Thus, a man standing on a completely flat plain with uninterrupted views to the horizon would be subject to 100 per cent daylight; any buildings or mountains restricting his view would reduce this figure.

The daylight available in a room is made up of three components:

(1)   sky component – luminance obtained directly from the sky;
(2)   externally reflected component – luminance reflected from external surfaces; and
(3)   internally reflected component – luminance reflected from internal surfaces.

The luminance from these three sources is added and the ratio of the total to the luminance of an unobstructed sky is the daylight factor. Luminance is measured in absolute quantities of lm/m^2. It is recommended that normal office workers require 10 lm/m^2 and drawing-office workers 45 lm/m^2. Since the luminance of the sky varies considerably according to the weather, it has been internationally agreed that the luminance of a completely overcast sky (CIE sky) should be taken as 500 lm/m^2. Thus, to have a luminance of 10 lm/m^2, an office would need to have a daylight factor of 2 per cent.

Daylight requirements for new buildings are laid down in the Department of the Environment's publication *Sunlight and Daylight*.[4] This recommends that daylight standards should be measured in terms only of the minimum 'sky component' at the building façade (the actual daylight factor may be two or three times the sky component, depending on the reflectance of internal and external surfaces). This minimum sky component must be present at all points above 2m from the ground. The recommended minima are as follows:

Residential buildings   0·84 per cent
Non-residential buildings 0·97 per cent

The sky component is not to be measured over the whole visual field. For each category of building, horizontal and vertical 'angles of acceptance' are defined; these describe an 'envelope' that admits 2·9 per cent of the sky's daylight for residential buildings, and 5·1 per cent for non-residential buildings. It follows that, without the daylight standards being infringed, this envelope can be up to 71 per cent obscured on the façade of residential buildings, and up to 81 per cent obscured on the façade of non-residential buildings.

Fig. 8.2 shows the proportion of the daylight envelope obscured by different types of overhead track placed parallel to, and at different distances from, the building line. The proportion of daylight envelope obscured must be measured at all points on the building façade 2−6m above ground level. Fig. 8.2 refers to the point above ground at which daylight is most obscured.

It can be seen that, at distances less than 6m from the building line,

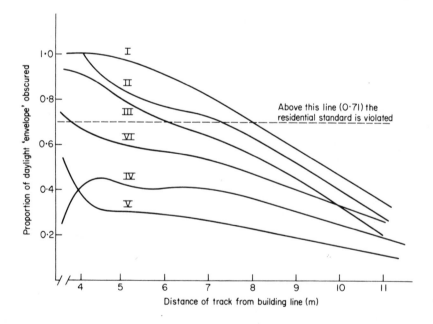

Fig. 8.2   Daylight

136

none of the 'sidewall' track systems is acceptable, and, using this criterion, the edge of a typical double autotram track would have to be placed at least 7·8m from the building line. Systems IV, V and VI all perform noticeably better than systems I, II and III; the less intrusive character of VI (4m wide) compared with III (2m wide) is a result of reducing track depth (0·6m compared with 1m), a more important factor than track width as far as daylight interference is concerned.

Double-track versions of IV and V do not need a continuous width of beam — there could be a break between the two tracks. However, having a gap between the tracks rather than a continuous wide beam does not increase the daylight received at a house façade, except where the track is placed very close to the façade (i.e. less than 4m away from it). In other words, occupiers of the houses affected would not be able to see the gap, and therefore such a system would appear to them to be like system VI.

Only in the widest streets (in excess of 34m between building lines, buildings 8m high) in the absence of any obstructions between building lines is the maximum daylight factor recorded. In streets of normal urban width (10–30m between building lines), the buildings on one side of the street obstruct the daylight received by buildings on the opposite side. This has to be taken into account when interpreting Fig. 8.2, and, as a result, the minimum distance of the track from the building line must be adjusted. Table 8.2 shows the minimum street widths that can accommodate the different track types, if daylight standards are to be satisfied.

Table 8.2

Implication of daylight standards:
street widths necessary to accommodate overhead track

| Track type | Residential areas (non-residential areas in brackets) | |
	Street width	Distance of nearside of track from building line
I	21 (16)	8 (5·5)
II	19 (14)	8 (5·5)
III	18 (13)	8 (5·5)
IV	9 (4)	9 (4)
V	9 (4)	9 (4)
VI	13 (4·5)	13 (4·5)

Sunlight

Daylight factors are a useful measure of the *quantity* of daylight available in rooms, and give some idea of the degree to which they are 'overlooked'. An indication of the *quality* of light available at a façade can be obtained by calculating how much sunlight would reach it.

When calculating hours of sunlight, more factors must be considered than when calculating the quantity of daylight. In addition to the dimensions of any obstruction and its orientation relative to the building façade (the factors that determine the sky component at a façade), the amount of sunlight that the façade will receive depends upon:

(1) the time of year;
(2) the latitude of the façade;
(3) the orientation of the façade (i.e. east, west, north, or south).

The effect on sunlight of placing different types of overhead structure at different distances from the façade was estimated by assuming, as was the case with the daylight calculations, that the track structure was placed parallel to the façade. The calculations were based on the situation at latitude 53°N in two seasons, midsummer and late winter (the dates chosen were 21 June and 1 March). The situation in late winter is almost reproduced in early autumn, and therefore the hours of sunlight achieved on 1 March and 21 June represent the range achieved over seven months of the year. The hours of sunlight for different orientations of the façade between due east and due west were considered.

The DOE publication *Daylight and Sunlight* recommends that the erection of buildings should take into account the amount of sunlight available on 1 March on all façades (excluding end walls less than 15m long) with a south-facing component. The DOE suggests that all points 2m or more above the ground should receive at least three hours sunlight during the time when the sun is at an elevation of 10° or more above the horizon. Thus, low-intensity sunlight, though at an elevation to cause discomfort, is excluded from the calculations (we have used the term 'useful sunlight' to denote light obtained from the sun when it has an elevation of 10° or more above the horizon).

Fig. 8.3 shows the amount of sunlight available at a façade if different types of track are placed at different distances away from it and it otherwise enjoys an uninterrupted view. On the vertical axis of the figure is shown the amount of sunlight received at the point, 2m or more above ground, that receives the least amount of sunlight. Track types I, III, V and VI are illustrated. For type I for a west-facing façade, the minimum

138

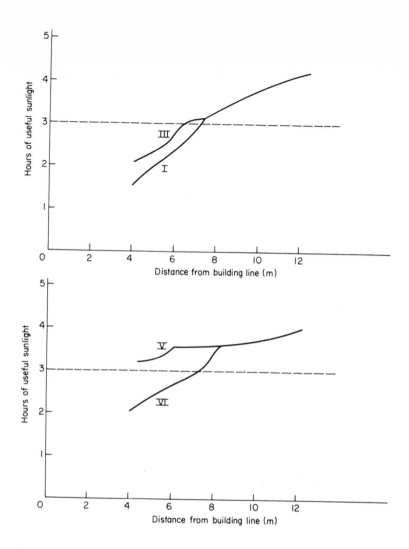

Fig. 8.3   Hours of sunlight (1 March, orientation west, 53°N)

distance that the track must be from the building line in order to satisfy the sunlight standards is 7·5m, and similar graphs can be constructed for other orientations. For instance, the minimum distance for type V, for any orientation south of east–west, is under 4m.

It might be asserted that the recommendations of *Daylight and Sunlight* are rather conservative, since sunlight standards need only be satisfied 2m or more above the ground; in most houses such a standard will not guarantee adequate sunlight in the ground-floor rooms where people spend most of the daylight hours. If the 'three hours of sun' standard is applied to the ground floor, then the minimum acceptable distance of the track from the building line is increased from nearly 6 to 8m for a type I structure for a south-east facing façade. For south-facing façades the minimum distance would be 9m.

Because the sun is higher in the sky at midsummer than it is in spring, overhead track structures create less obstruction at that time of year. Again, the amount of obstruction varies with the orientation of the building: south-facing façades suffer no loss of sunlight at all, even where structures are placed only 4m away from them; and on west-facing façades a type I system obstructs no more than 1·5 hours of useful sunlight – again, even if the track is placed only 4m away.

Just as the amount of daylight enjoyed by buildings on one side of a street may be restricted by buildings on the other side, so too may the amount of sunlight be restricted; and thus the maximum acceptable distance between the track and the building line is increased. Table 8.3 gives the minimum street widths necessary, under the DOE recommendations referred to above, to accommodate the different types of track. It is assumed that the track is placed along streets with façades 8m high. If sunlight criteria are to be based on the amount of sun available at ground-floor level, then the minimum street widths are increased by up to 7m, depending upon orientation.

Table 8.3

Implication of sunlight standards:
street widths necessary to accommodate elevated track

Building-line orientation	Track type	Street width	Distance of track from building line
West	I	21	8
	III	18	8
	V	16	7·5
	VI	19	7·5
South	I	20	7·5
	III	17	7·5
	V	15	7
	VI	18	7
South-east	I	16	5·5
	III	13	5·5
	V	11	5
	VI	14	5

A comparison of Tables 8.2 and 8.3 shows that, for west-facing façades, the sunlight and daylight standards give identical results for trough-type tracks: a minimum street width of 21m for a double-track wide-vehicle system and 18m for a single-track narrow-vehicle system. For south and south-east facing façades, the daylight standard provides the more severe constraint, except in the case of the suspended type V and the centre-guidance system type VI, for which sunlight standards provide a more severe constraint for all orientations of the façade.

Combining the two constraints, we may say that the absolute minimum street width that satisfies both daylight and sunlight criteria is 21m for a double-track sidewall system and 14–19m for a centre-guidance system – depending upon orientation. For reasons explained above, a double-track suspended system would have a very similar impact to a double-track centre-guidance system.

Noise

Since the publication of the Wilson Report,[5] it has become accepted in official circles that the noise implications of proposed developments (particularly transport developments) should be taken seriously at planning and development stage. Noise can be defined here as 'unwanted sound'.

The common unit for measuring sound is the decibel *(dB)*. This, strictly speaking, is a measure of sound pressure, and is arrived at by means of a logarithmic transformation of a linear scale of pressure. The sound pressure level is calculated according to the formula $dB = 20 \log_{10} \frac{r_i}{r_o}$, where r_i is the sound pressure level measured on an arithmetic scale, and r_o is the reference pressure level (usually $2 \times 10^{-5} N/m^2$). Since $\log_{10} 2 = \cdot 3010$, a doubling of sound pressure is approximately re-presented by an increase of *6dB* (20 x ·3010).

It has been found that annoyance is related not only to sound pressure, but also to sound frequency (other things being equal, low-frequency sounds are less annoying than high-frequency sounds). Most sound sources encountered in everyday life emit a complex sound made up of different frequencies. The overall sound pressure level is simply the arithmetic sum of the sound pressures (converted to decibels) recorded in each frequency band. An alternative measure is the *dB(A)*. With this the sound pressure level in each frequency band is weighted in proportion to the annoyance caused by that particular frequency. The sound level in *dB(A)* is the logarithmic transformation of the sum. The *dB(A)* is usually used when assessing the level of annoyance of a sound. Experiments have shown that people associate a doubling in the loudness of a sound with an increase of $10dB(A)$.

At a fixed measuring point, the sound level due to the passage of a stream of vehicles changes constantly, as the position of all vehicles in the stream changes relative to the measuring point. The position is illustrated in Fig. 8.4, where it is assumed that vehicles follow each other at a constant headway. If the rate of dissipation follows the inverse-square law, the maximum noise level (L_{max}) occurs when the vehicle that makes the major contribution to the noise level is directly opposite O, the measuring point. Similarly, it can be shown that the minimum noise level will be experienced when the distance from the measuring point to the nearest vehicle is at a maximum. Other measures of the noise level may be calculated by similar methods; thus, the noise level exceeded for 50 per cent of the time occurs when the nearest vehicle is at a point $\frac{\cdot 5H}{2}$ from the line OP, while the noise level exceeded for 10 per cent of the time is experienced when the nearest vehicle is at a distance $\frac{1H}{2}$ from OP. Given the assumption that vehicles are spread regularly along the track, it is possible to calculate the temporal distribution of noise levels at any point, provided the noise of the individual vehicle (usually given in terms of the sound level measured at a particular distance from the vehicle) is known. Blitz[6] has produced a simple method of calculating the temporal distribution of noise levels, and it is on this that the present analysis of noise from reserved-track systems is based.

Criteria for assessing noise levels. The noise standards that have been suggested in different countries to regulate road traffic noise are mostly based on L_{10} levels. (In addition, of course, most countries impose maximum standards on individual vehicles; in the United Kingdom, these standards are contained in the Vehicle Construction and Use Regulations.) The only statutory regulations that can be applied to noise from reserved-track systems are those contained in orders carried under the 1973 Land Compensation Act. The Act was intended to protect occupiers from the adverse effects of new road construction and states that they are entitled to a statutory right of compensation where the sound level from traffic using a new or improved road exceeds $68dB(A)$ (this being the L_{10} level measured over an 18-hour day).

These standards appear to be on the conservative side. Surveys of people's reaction to road traffic noise have suggested that, when the L_{10} level from road traffic is around $70dB(A)$, then 50 per cent of the population are 'satisfied' with the noise level and 50 per cent 'dissatisfied'.[7] Therefore, if the noise level produced by an automatic

142

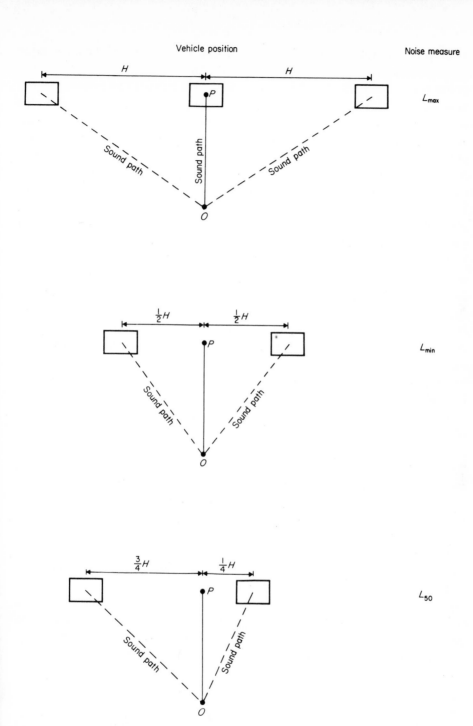

Fig. 8.4   Distribution of noise levels

system is $68dB(A)$, we could expect nearly 50 per cent of the population to be considerably disturbed as a result. The $68dB(A)$ level represents a compromise between what society wants and what it can achieve in the near future with the existing state of motor-vehicle technology. For this reason, it might be expected that automatic systems being designed from scratch would be expected to satisfy more rigorous standards. It is usually considered that ideal standards are represented by the Wilson Report,[8] which suggests that in urban areas the L_{10} levels inside houses should not exceed $50\ dB(A)$ during the day. The normal façade of a house with windows 'partly open' provides $10dB(A)$ insulation;[9] thus, if the L_{10} level measured externally does not exceed $60dB(A)$ then the internal level will satisfy the Wilson standard.

L_{10} levels are appropriate bases for standards only when the service interval between vehicles is small — as is the case with busy roads. In such cases, there is only a small difference between the maximum noise level (L_{max}) and the L_{10} level, and, therefore, if the L_{10} standard is satisfied, it is unlikely that the maximum noise will be unduly disturbing. However, where there is a large service interval between vehicles, the L_{10} standards do not guarantee that L_{max} is tolerable. Thus, aircraft noise control is based on L_{max} and not L_{10}. Since autotram may operate at quite long headways, it is desirable to propose both a maximum noise level and a standard based on the level not to be exceeded for more than 10 per cent of the time. No such standards with respect to vehicle noise have been suggested. However, a series of experiments at the Motor Industry Research Association revealed that, where the noise of a single passing car was $75dB(A)$, then, for a sample population, the number of people satisfied by the noise was the same as the number dissatisfied. We adopted this as a maximum standard for a single autotram vehicle. This leads to a two-tier standard: namely, that the noise level from a stream of autotram vehicles should not exceed $68dB(A)$ for more than 10 per cent of the time, nor should the sound from an individual vehicle exceed $75dB(A)$.

Fig. 8.5 shows the L_{10} levels that would be produced by a line of autotram vehicles operating at a frequency and speed similar to that envisaged in the Coventry study (20 seconds, 54 km/h). L_{10} levels were calculated for vehicles with three different reference sound levels — 75, 70, 65 — and are shown for different distances from the track centreline.

An alternative way of looking at the problem is to ask what the reference sound level would have to be if a particular standard were to be satisfied. The lower diagram shows what the implications of the two-tier standard referred to earlier would be for systems operating at different service intervals. On the horizontal axis is shown the distance of the track

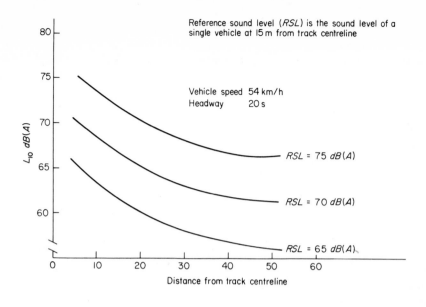

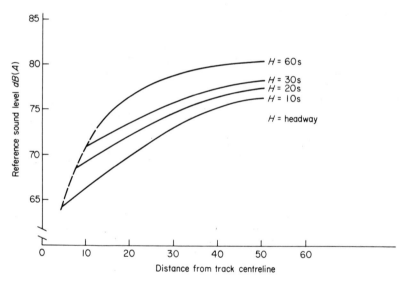

Fig. 8.5 Noise levels of autotram

centreline from the building façade, at which point the standard must be
achieved, and on the vertical axis is shown the reference sound level
necessary to achieve that standard. Four different headways are shown —
10, 20, 30, and 60 seconds. Where the graph is broken the maximum noise

level is the effective constraint; where the line is solid the L_{10} level is the effective constraint.

Fig. 8.5 also shows the L_{10} levels that would be produced by two lines of autotram vehicles (double track). The maximum noise level in this situation will occur when two vehicles are passing and, in order to take account of this, the dotted line in the lower diagram should be moved to the right.

Since automatic transport vehicle technology is in its infancy, it is hardly surprising that information on likely noise levels is scanty; even where prototype vehicles exist, manufacturers tend to be reluctant to release information on noise. Four automatic transport systems were exhibited at the Transpo '72 exhibition and their exterior noise levels were recorded at a distance of 7·6m from the track centreline. Table 8.4 gives the results from the noise-testing programme; the sound levels measured have been adjusted to a distance of 15m from the centreline (it is assumed that noise decays at a rate of $6dB$ for each doubling of distance). In the rest of this book the sound level at 15m from the track centreline will be referred to as the reference level of the system.

Table 8.4

Reference sound levels for Transpo systems

System	Line speed (km/hour)	Propulsion system	Suspension system	Reference noise level: $dB(A)$ at 15m
Dashaveyor (Bendix)	26	DC rotary motor	Wheels	64
ACT (Ford)	19	DC rotary motor induction	Wheels	69
Hovair (Otis)	22	Linear induction motor	Air pads	60
Monocab (Rohr)	16	DC rotary motor	Wheels	59

The first three systems in the table are bottom-supported systems relying on sidewall guidance; the sound-level readings were taken with the microphone 1–2m above ground. Monocab is a suspended system, and the sound-level readings were taken at the same level as the track, 7·6m above the ground. It should be emphasised that the noise levels correspond to quite low line speeds. At normal operating speeds (40–60 km/h), noise levels might be 5–10dB higher. Noise levels would also be higher during periods of acceleration and deceleration.

The reference sound level for a stationary Urba vehicle, powered by linear motors, and having an air-pad suspension system, is reliably reported as 62dB(A). [10] In view of its propulsion and suspension system this might be taken as representative of the sound level while in motion.

If autotram is to avoid creating excessive noise in urban areas, its reference sound level should not exceed 65dB(A) — the American Department of Transportation actually recommends a maximum of 57dB(A) at 8m. It would then easily satisfy the two-tier standard outlined above and, from the viewpoint of noise, there should be no great objection to placing a double track as near as 10m to building façades. In most cases such a reference level would cause little nuisance and with the track placed more than 20m from the façade would not violate the Wilson standards. However, to achieve a reference sound level of 65dB(A), sound insulation on and off the vehicle may be necessary, and in the case of steel wheels this may be difficult and expensive to achieve.

Impact of ground-level track

The environmental costs of ground-level track are no greater than they would be if the same land were used for a road — indeed, they are likely to be lower, since autotram vehicles would not be responsible for roadside pollution and would be quieter than motor cars. However, opportunity costs are considerable where there is competition for the use of the land. It may be possible to locate routes in places where the opportunity cost of the land is low: for instance, by the side of railway lines or along the route of an abandoned railway line; but such opportunities are not always available. This means that, if acquisition of residential properties is ruled out, the systems must use the only other available corridors — roads.

The use of highways imposes costs on existing highway users — both pedestrians and vehicle users. An autotram system does not only remove from its existing use land devoted to the passage of pedestrians and vehicles, but also creates the effect commonly known as 'severance', by establishing through the city a series of physical barriers difficult to cross. This is less of a sacrifice where the system runs along a major road, in which case high traffic volumes have already created an element of neighbourhood severance; but it is particularly serious when the roads concerned are minor roads where traffic is light, and streets that behave as neighbourhoods.

Minimum road and pavement widths

The Ministry of Transport publication *Roads in Urban Areas* [11] lays down the desirable minimum widths for different categories of urban roads. Such standards are not always satisfied by existing roads, but, of course, are expected to be satisfied by any new roads. It might also be assumed that, where these standards are not satisfied, the situation should not deteriorate further.

The minimum width for a highway is the minimum width for the roadway plus the minimum width for each pavement. On primary and district distributors, it is reasonable to assume that the width reserved for vehicles must be at least 7·4m, allowing one stream of vehicles to pass in each direction. According to *Roads in Urban Areas,* the minimum pavement width for such roads should be 2·7m, but in urban areas narrower pavements are commonly accepted, and it would be possible to reduce the minimum width to 1·9m if required. This means that the minimum width to be available for the passing and repassing of vehicles and pedestrians on a primary distributor road is 11·2m.

The minimum roadway width for local access and local distributor roads might be as little as 3·9m. This allows the passage of two streams of cars, though, if the road is to be used for heavy vehicles, it would have to be turned into a one-way street. Again, 1·9m wide pavements are required to serve developments on both sides of this road, bringing the minimum road width on local access and local distributor roads to 7·7m. Table 8.5 gives the minimum highway width required to accommodate ground-level track, and the same requirements hold for partially submerged track. The table assumes that 0·3m horizontal clearance must be maintained between autotrams on adjacent tracks, between autotrams and the edge of the right of way, and between the right of way and the roadway used by other vehicles. These dimensions represent the absolute minimum width necessary if a road is to carry out its functions as a traffic artery. Two assumptions, both of them open to challenge, are made here:

(1)   that it is possible, on an-all purpose street, to build the track along the side of the roadway;
(2)   that a dual carriageway may be created, with carriageways only 3·7m wide.

If the track is built along the side of a roadway, then vehicular access is entirely denied to one side of the street. A dual carriageway with carriageways 3·7m wide will not function as efficiently as a single carriageway 7·4m wide. Ideally, each carriageway should be wide enough to permit two vehicles to pass one another. This would mean that each carriageway should be 6m wide − leading to desirable road widths considerably in excess of those given in Table 8.5. The requirement that

148

Table 8.5

Recommended highway widths (m)

Vehicle width	Single-track	Double-track
	Primary and district distributors	
1·4	14·2	15·9
2·0	14·8	17·1
	Local distributors and access roads	
1·4	10·7	12·4
2·0	11·3	14·1

vehicular access be preserved along the roadside on local access roads would similarly increase the minimum widths. Fig. 8.6 shows two possible street cross-sections that result from applying these standards.

Where ground-level track runs along primary and district distributors, it is unlikely that it would be acceptable to block off junctions between one such road and another of the same category. Consequently, it would be necessary for the track to pass either below or above the existing traffic, and in most such cases it would be necessary to tunnel beneath the other road. We considered what length of tunnel and cutting would be required and found that the major constraint would be that imposed by other vehicular traffic: it is desirable to maintain the original roadway width not only at the junction itself, but also at the junction approaches, enabling right-turning traffic to queue at the junction approach and not block other traffic while waiting to manoeuvre.

Implications of standards

The standards discussed so far cover only a few of the issues that would have to be considered in a detailed study of a particular autotram route. However, we may use them to get some idea of the magnitude of the problems involved in fitting an autotram system into an existing city. We decided to see whether it was possible to build an autotram route in Coventry without infringing these standards, and without having to resort to the acquisition of private property.

Since Coventry's transport, both passenger and goods, has been almost

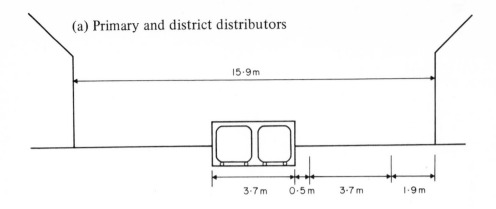

(a) Primary and district distributors

15·9 m

3·7 m   0·5 m   3·7 m   1·9 m

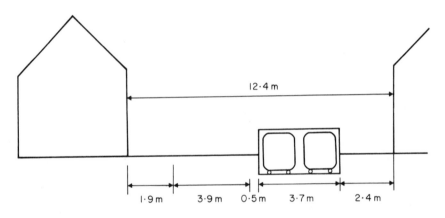

(b) Local distributors and access roads

12·4 m

1·9 m   3·9 m   0·5 m   3·7 m   2·4 m

Fig. 8.6   Minimum highway cross-section for partially submerged track

entirely road-based, and movement has been radial, activity tends to concentrate at the centre and along the radial roads, which also provide a good, usually straight, uninterrupted right of way from the suburbs to the fringes of the central area. For these reasons we first investigated the feasibility of building the tracks along existing radial roads.

Fig. 8.7 shows those radial roads where it would be 'not unacceptable' to build an overhead system of 5m double-track width. In general, it is difficult to approach within 2km of the city centre. Opportunities to the north of the city are more restricted than elsewhere, and it does not seem acceptable to use elevated track along the northern corridor. The areas

150

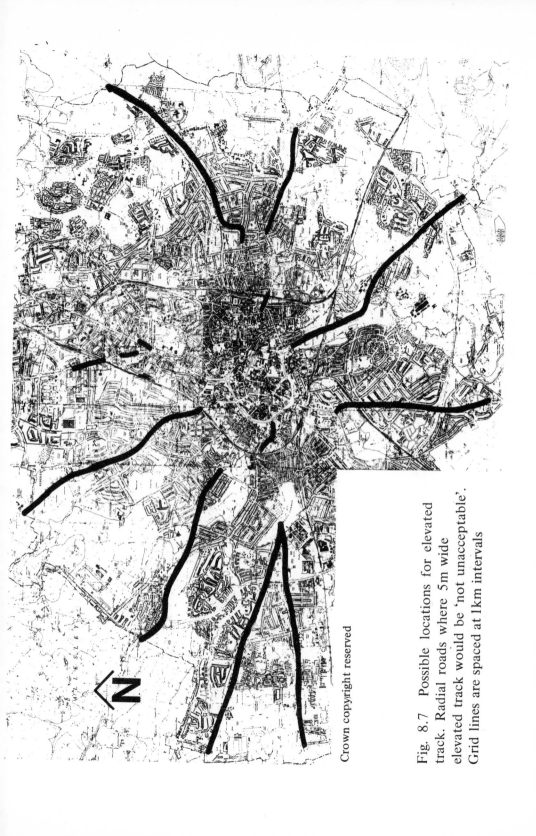

Crown copyright reserved

Fig. 8.7 Possible locations for elevated track. Radial roads where 5m wide elevated track would be 'not unacceptable'. Grid lines are spaced at 1km intervals

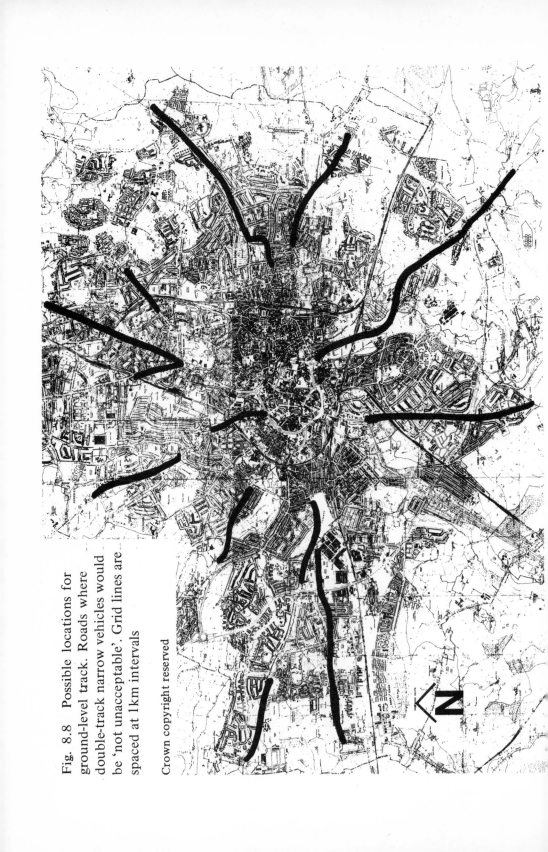

Fig. 8.8 Possible locations for ground-level track. Roads where double-track narrow vehicles would be 'not unacceptable'. Grid lines are spaced at 1km intervals

Crown copyright reserved

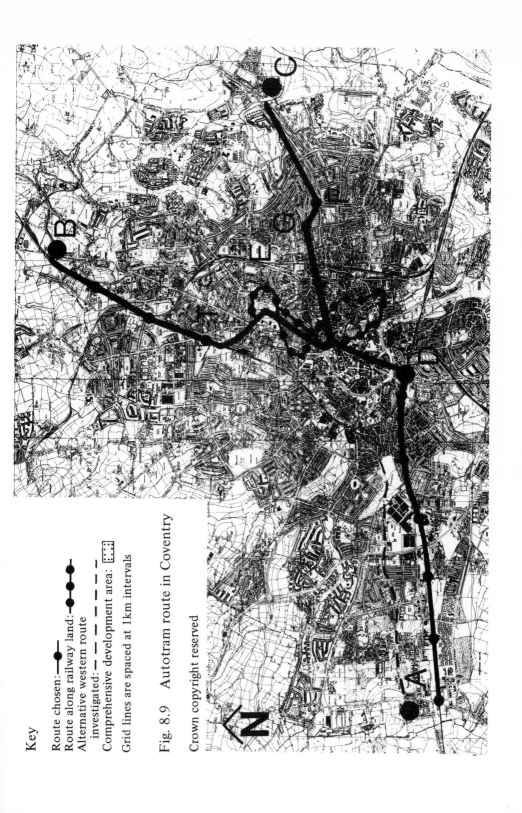

Key

Route chosen: ●━━●
Route along railway land: ━━●●━━
Alternative western route
  investigated: ━ ━ ━
Comprehensive development area: ⬚
Grid lines are spaced at 1 km intervals

Fig. 8.9 Autotram route in Coventry

Crown copyright reserved

where overhead track is 'not unacceptable' can be roughly described as those where the roads were built up after 1918 and typical net residential densities are less than 37 dwellings per hectare. A brief examination of the widths of roads in Coventry was sufficient to suggest that ground-level track along existing rights of way would not be possible with 2m-wide vehicles, and therefore only the limits of penetration of 1·4m-wide vehicles were investigated. The roads that could accommodate such vehicles are shown in Fig. 8.8. There is marginally better penetration of the area at ground level than overhead, but, again, penetration from the north by a double-track system laid along existing roads would be impossible, and track along the north-east corridor would have to go underground within 2km of the city centre. At first sight, therefore, it might appear that an autotram system could be built, either overhead or at ground level, using extensive lengths of existing streets. However, other factors are likely to reduce the acceptability of such systems along existing rights of way. One inhibiting factor will be the effects of both ground-level and overhead systems on existing traffic.

Along most of the streets where it is shown in Figs. 8.7 and 8.8 that elevated or ground-level track is 'not unacceptable' this is possible only if the track is built in the centre of the roadway. Only thus can elevated track be placed sufficiently far from housing to satisfy daylight and sunlight regulations, and ground-level track be placed in such a way as to permit unimpaired access to frontages. Over most of the roads this means creating a dual carriageway from a single carriageway. Unfortunately, only along very short sections of road would it be possible to create two 6m carriageways from an existing single-carriageway road and at the same time avoid enlarging the highway by encroaching on private land.

A second inhibiting factor that must be taken into account is the visual effect of the new track structures. Although it is not possible to draw up rules to give aesthetic judgements, and equally impossible here to give a street-by-street account of the visual effects of autotram in Coventry, it cannot be denied that the kind of elevated structures required by an autotram system are massive and inclined to dominate the scene when placed in areas of low-density housing. In their study of Minitram in Sheffield,[12] Robert Matthew, Johnson-Marshall and Partners assert that it is possible to overcome the problems posed by the relatively large size of guideways by reducing them in height, so that they are less oppressive and more in scale with surrounding buildings and spaces. However, an opportunity to reduce the height of elevated structures is likely to exist only in pedestrian precincts, or where track may be built along wide sections of central reservation. Unfortunately, such opportunities are rare outside the central area: most roads are single carriageways, and all fulfil important traffic functions.

The aesthetic acceptability of overhead track is partly determined by the degree of compatibility between the overhead structures and surrounding buildings. The uncompromising nature of the track structure is likely to be most compatible with modern city centres, and most jarring in quiet residential streets. Here the very motion of the vehicles is an intrusion on the quietness of the neighbourhood, while the track structure is out of sympathy with the surrounding buildings. Clearly, the movement of the vehicles would not in itself be upsetting on major radial roads, but, except with very wide roads, there would tend to be a clash in scale between the track and surrounding development. This is because development outside the inner core of a city is usually limited to buildings of two storeys.

Route selection for the three Coventry corridors

Fig. 8.9 shows the route alignment finally chosen for the three corridors discussed in Chapter 7. The basic problem is to link points A, B and C with point D (the railway station).

From our analysis of the public-health constraints and our general consideration of environmental factors, it appeared that use of existing streets would be impossible along the northern corridor (the line BD) and merely difficult on the western (AD) and north-eastern (CD) corridors. Thus it appeared necessary to examine the possibility of locating the track where it was less likely to cause offence – in particular, by using land alongside railway lines and within comprehensive development areas (CDAs).

Extensive use could be made of both CDA and railway land to overcome the problems of route penetration along the northern corridor. There is no abandoned railway that might be used, but there is an existing goods line that links Coventry and Nuneaton, and enough spare land along the side of it to accommodate a double autotram track. The shaded areas on Fig. 8.9 indicate areas of comprehensive redevelopment. Use of the Eagle Street and Red Lane CDA (marked E) enables the route to reach the inner Coventry ring road entirely at ground level; this only leaves an area, between the Red Lane CDA and the Nuneaton railway line, occupied by a large textile firm (marked T). This is the 'pinch point' of the northern section: the track has to pass behind a series of gardens, along a factory road, and over the A444 road. This should be possible even with wide vehicles, but fairly tight radii of curvature are needed (no more than 20m).

The western corridor first passes through an area of Edwardian artisan housing, then through low-density inter-war and post-war residential estates. A reserved-track route would also serve a number of industrial sites, including two large vehicle factories. Reference to Figs. 8.7 and 8.8 shows that it would be theoretically possible to build either a ground-level or elevated track along the roads that serve the corridor. However, the construction of ground-level track involves a considerable sacrifice of road capacity — in few places could the ideal 6m roadway width be maintained on both sides of the carriageways. The railway in this corridor is the section of the main Euston–Birmingham line that lies between Tile Hill station and Coventry station. Open land exists beside this line, and the route would be 'easy' to about halfway, after which the line enters a cutting; but between there and the station there is space enough to build a track along the top of the cutting and along the fringes of a park. It has been proposed that the existing double-track railway will be turned into a four-track line after the introduction of the Advanced Passenger Train; should this happen, it would make little difference to the first half of the route, but over the second half there would hardly be enough land to accommodate an autotram route.

There is no railway right of way that can be exploited along the north-east corridor, and therefore most of the track would have to pass along existing routes, either at ground level or overhead. Between points C and F a dual carriageway can be used, but beyond point F the street system can no longer be satisfactorily used either for ground-level or overhead track. Reference to Fig. 8.7 shows that overhead track could be continued slightly further without infringing public-health standards, but the distance between building lines narrows beyond point F, and the 'wide-open-space' feeling that characterises the dual-carriageway section and might absorb the massiveness of the overhead track has disappeared. Fig. 8.9 shows the track crossing open space beyond point F (the land is currently used as allotment gardens). Beyond Point G the track has to be constructed underground, though the section through the Hillfields CDA could be built at ground level.

The central area

Fewer constraints apply to construction in the central area, because most of the buildings are not used for residential purposes. Moreover, elevated track is more likely to be compatible with the scale of buildings there than

156

in the residential areas. However, all three routes have to enter the central area via a tunnel: access from the North is blocked by the elevated ring road; and the western route approaches the central area via the railway station. The station area is becoming an area of high office blocks, and it is very difficult to find an elevated route across it.

It is theoretically possible to bring routes up to ground level again and take the routes across the town at roof level, but there seems to be much to recommend continuing the route in a tunnel.

The accommodation of stations

Along most of the route, station location does not present too much of a problem, provided island platforms are used. It is even possible to fit in such a station at ground level on the dual-carriageway section of the north-eastern corridor. One station has to be built elevated: that by the textile factory on the northern corridor. Such a structure might well be compatible with the massiveness of the textile factory, but in residential areas elevated stations would be overbearing in relation to their surroundings.

Within the city boundary, the distribution of the various types of construction is as follows:

	Double-track km	Percentage of total
Ground level	21·6	62
Elevated	10·2	29
Underground	3·2	9
Total	35·0	100

It would appear that in Coventry the opportunities for running track along existing rights of way are few — even if only the crudest public-health standards are invoked against overhead track. The route in Coventry would involve many changes of level and the use of tight radii of curvature, which would not be possible with a conventional railway. Even along railway land both elevated and ground-level track would have to be used, with frequent changes over short distances in the type of track employed. Thus, although, in the case of Coventry, some of the more extravagant claims for the system's adaptability do not appear to be justified, it remains true that autotram can succeed in providing reserved-track facilities where more conventional systems would fail.

Notes

[1] For a detailed account of this matter see John R. Kellet, *Impact of Railways on Victorian Cities,* Routledge and Kegan Paul, 1969.

[2] See B. Grant and W. Russell, *Opportunities in Automated Urban Transport,* 1973, available from Robert Matthew, Johnson-Marshall and Partners, Welwyn Garden City.

[3] Cutmone, *Shaw's Commentary on the Building Regulations,* Shaw and Sons, 1965.

[4] *Daylight and Sunlight,* HMSO, 1971.

[5] *Noise,* Final Report, HMSO, 1963.

[6] J. Blitz 'Prediction of L_{10} on urban main roads', *Acustica* vol. 29, S. Hirzel Verlag, Stuttgart 1973.

[7] I.D. Griffiths and F.S. Langdon, *Subjective Response to Road Traffic Noise,* Building Research Station Current Paper 37/68, Ministry of Public Building and Works, 1968.

[8] *Noise,* op.cit.

[9] *Noise,* op.cit., Appendix.

[10] Derived from data presented in J.W. Fitchie, 'The problems of financing transport systems', *Aeronautical Journal,* April 1973.

[11] *Roads in Urban Areas,* HMSO, 1963.

[12] *Minitram in Sheffield,* Robert Matthew, Johnson-Marshall and Partners, 1974.

9 The Rôle of Autotram

This chapter examines the future prospects of automated transport in the light of the study in Coventry and other evidence. Economic and environmental factors are constraints that limit the area of applicability of automated transport, and in this chapter the relevance of the economic constraint is considered first. This is followed by an examination of the environmental constraint, to see whether installations that might be acceptable on economic grounds are likely to prove unacceptable when the wider considerations of their effect on the environment and of non-user reaction to them are taken into account.

In looking at the problem in this way, we are attempting to identify where and when automated transport will prove superior to the best that conventional transport modes can offer. By examining automated transport in different places — cities with different patterns of transport demand and different transport networks — it should be possible to identify the factors that are critical to the viability of the mode. These factors include elements of cost and performance in different situations, and the alternatives available. The aim is to find the combination of parameters (or factors) that defines the frontier between success and failure.

Costs and performance of autotram

The decision to install a section of autotram route will depend to some extent on the economic costs of building and operating it, and the benefits to be derived by passengers. In the planning stage these will be compared with various alternatives, which in most British towns will mean buses or, occasionally, a railway.

The Coventry study found the total cost (i.e. capital plus operating costs) of autotram to be 3·1p per passenger km, but this figure may change considerably with the type of route and the level of demand. A cost is usually defined as 'capital' or 'operating' on the basis of whether it is a once-and-for-all expenditure or recurs over time at regular intervals. Thus, the costs of providing track and station structures, with an assumed life of 25 years, would be classed as capital expenditure, and expenditure on power, maintenance and management would be classed as operating expenses. Less easy to define are the costs incurred in purchasing vehicles, which have a life of between eight and nine years (700,000 km was the assumed life in the Coventry study). Many accountants may prefer to place expenditure on them in the capital account, but, because we preferred to define capital expenditure as expenditure independent of the level of passenger demand, we chose to include them under operating expenses. The remaining expenditure (operating costs) is then a linear function of demand. In other words, capital expenditure on track, stations and control is the same for a given route regardless of the level of passenger demand. This is a slight oversimplification, since the size of the maintenance area is influenced by the number of vehicles (and hence passenger demand), the size of stations is partly determined by the level of expected demand, and the control system' may be more or less sophisticated depending on the passenger capacity required. On the whole, though, the original claim that capital costs are independent of passenger demand is a close-enough approximation for our purposes. The statement that operating costs are a simple multiple of passenger demand is also violated, though not seriously, in one or two instances. Central management is one example where the rule may not apply, and some maintenance expenditure (on track, for instance) may be dependent on the passage of time rather than on the passage of vehicles and passengers.

Fig. 9.1 describes the situation on the basis of this distinction between the two types of cost; the cost assumptions are those of Chapter 7. As passenger demand increases, the fixed capital cost is shared among more people and the cost per passenger falls, approaching, but never reaching, the (constant) level of operating costs per passenger km (1·9p). The capital cost varies with the type of route. It is at a maximum when all the route is underground, and at a minimum when the route is entirely at ground level. Under most circumstances, the cost will fall between the two extremes. The situation found in the Coventry study is also shown. The costs per passenger km are calculated from the total passenger demand per annum, and the two other scales — average link demand in the peak hours, and maximum link demand in the peak half-hour — are based on Coventry conditions. Other towns may show a greater or lesser tendency to peak in both time and place. Whatever the details of cost and demand, the message of the graph is clear: as demand increases, the average cost per passenger falls.

If we turn to the performance of autotram and the benefits to passengers, we see that the picture is complex here as well. We have already shown that station spacing is an optimisation problem in which the objective is to balance the benefits derived from short walks to the

160

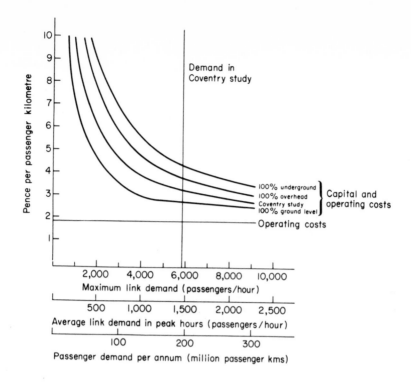

Fig. 9.1   Cost per passenger with different assumptions about track and passenger demand (1973 prices)

station against increased cost and lower journey speeds. We also argued that optimum station spacing was likely to be about 600–700m for a level of demand similar to that found in Coventry. Some authorities might reject this argument and expect spacings nearer 400m, as generally found on bus routes. (It is assumed in this context that autotram is providing a comprehensive service for all public transport trips in the corridor under study, and that there is no parallel service — for instance, a bus or a suburban rail service — providing for either short trips or long trips). This dilemma cannot be avoided by adopting vehicles with a high cruise speed. In fact, the effect of increasing cruise speed (with acceleration and deceleration fixed by passenger-comfort criteria) would be to increase the optimum station spacing, as the time that passengers already on the vehicle would lose by stopping at a station would be increased. There are no firm guidelines for choosing the vehicle cruise speed, but in urban conditions it is unlikely that a speed in excess of 60km/h (16·7m/s) could be justified. In practice, the need to negotiate frequent curves, the extra

161

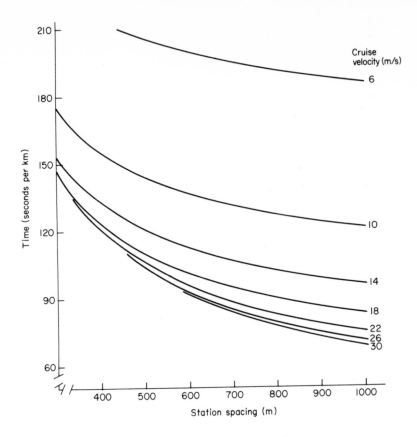

The time taken for a vehicle to travel one metre is given by

$$T = \frac{S+F}{SV}, \quad F = \frac{V^2}{2A} + \frac{V^2}{2D} + VL$$

where S = distance between stations (m)
         V = cruise velocity (m/s)
         A,D = rate of acceleration/deceleration (m^2/s)
         L = dwell time in stations (s)

Assumptions used for graph: $A,D = 1\cdot5$, $L = 15$

Fig. 9.2   The relationship between station spacing, journey time and cruise velocity

energy consumed, the increased stresses on the vehicle, and the tendency for time saved per unit increase in speed to fall will probably keep the most suitable cruise speed to around 50km/h (13·9m/s). Fig. 9.2 shows the effect on time per km travelled of variations in station spacing and cruise speed.

162

We can assume that waiting times on an autotram route will be low. Even with low levels of passenger demand, it would be possible to keep waiting times as low as one minute by reducing vehicle size. It may also be possible to join vehicles in the peak period and separate them in the off-peak, thus allowing frequencies to be kept approximately the same throughout the day.

Conversely, reliability should be high, the absence of shared rights of way and the existence of a central control ensuring that the service is regular. On the other hand, though, breakdowns of either the vehicles or the control system may cause serious disruption.

In the difficult area of comfort and convenience, it appears that autotram may have some advantages over conventional transport. These, however, are often exaggerated and do not comprise a major benefit of the system.

The rest of this section is devoted to a comparison between autotram and the other forms of urban public transport.

The comparison with buses

Statistics from the trading accounts[1] of municipal bus operators in the UK suggest that the cost of carrying passengers in 1973 varied between 1·4 and 1·9p per passenger km. The cost per passenger km travelled on buses is therefore not only below the total cost per passenger km on autotram, but even below the operating cost; but this is counterbalanced to some extent by the inferior level of service. Average journey speeds by bus are likely to be low (between 12 and 20 km per hour), and waiting times are likely to be quite long, especially where demand is low and buses are large. The walk to the nearest boarding point may be shorter than that suggested for autotram, but reliability and regularity of service will suffer from adverse traffic conditions. Whether the case is in favour of autotram or bus depends on the weight put on speed and reliability. In Coventry we found that the economic case was in the balance.

The trend of costs and benefits

When comparing with alternatives the effect of a proposed investment with a life of 20 or more years, it is necessary to consider not only its relative merits in the first year of installation, but also the trend in its advantage (or disadvantage). In the comparison between autotram and bus, there seem to be strong grounds for expecting the movement in costs and benefits over time to favour autotram.

To take benefits first, we saw that autotram has the potential to

163

provide a superior service, although at greater money cost. The superiority of the service takes the form of time saved: if people's valuation of time were to increase, and the relative money costs of the two modes were to remain the same, then this would be a movement in favour of autotram. Research has provided strong evidence that people's valuation of time does in fact increase as incomes increase. The Department of the Environment has accepted this finding, and recommends that in cost-benefit analyses the value of time (in real terms) should increase at 3¼ per cent a year in line with the expected increase in average earnings.

Turning to costs, there also appears to be a trend in favour of autotram. Fig. 9.3 gives some indices of earnings and prices during the period 1955–73 in the UK. During that period, average earnings per employed person rose on average by 7·6 per cent a year, and the price index of all goods and services rose by 4·2 per cent a year. The difference between the

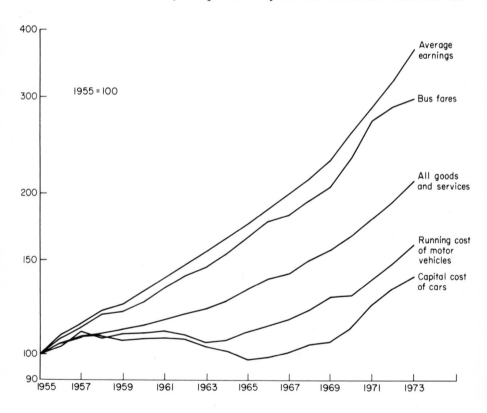

Fig. 9.3   The movement of earnings and prices in the UK, 1955–73
Source: *National Income and Expenditure.* Statistics adjusted for changes in rate of indirect taxation

164

two rates of growth reflects the change in the material standard of living, resulting from improvements in productivity per man. Over time each person (on average) produces more and more goods and services during a working day, due to the adoption of better processes of production, new goods, and improved methods of industrial organisation — in short, technical progress. Other factors — such as the ratio of import to export prices, accumulation of capital, indirect taxation, and changes in working hours — can influence the gap; but overwhelmingly it is technical progress, in the widest sense of the word, that is the major influence.

The average earnings of employees in road passenger transport during the same period increased at almost exactly the same rate as average earnings in the rest of the economy (7·6 per cent), but prices in this industry increased much faster (6·3 per cent). If prices had accurately reflected the rise in costs, the increase would have been about 7 per cent, but during the 1970s there was an increasing tendency for local authorities to grant bus operators revenue subsidies, thereby helping to mitigate the rise in prices. What the figures do show is that the improvement in productivity in bus operation has been low (between 0·5 and 1 per cent a year) compared with the case in the rest of the economy (where it has been over 3 per cent a year). The trends in the cost of purchasing and running cars provides an interesting comparison: the running costs of motor vehicles have risen by 2·7 per cent a year and the cost of new motor cars by 1·9 per cent a year, suggesting productivity improvements of 4·9 per cent and 5·5 per cent respectively. (The limited effect that changes in indirect taxation have had on prices has been excluded from these indices.)

Why has there been a different trend in the price of the two modes of transport, and can we derive any conclusions about the trend in productivity improvements and costs that autotram might enjoy? Over 70 per cent of the operating costs of buses are direct labour costs and, although a high proportion of labour costs in total costs does not in itself mean a low rate of productivity growth, it does in this case seem to reflect the core of the problem facing any attempt to improve productivity in the bus industry. The use of larger buses and the introduction of one-man operation have undoubtedly yielded improvements in productivity, but neither of these changes can guarantee continuous improvements. Improvements in vehicle design, operation and maintenance (common to cars as well) should continue to make a contribution towards increasing productivity, but it is in the area of the driver that productivity improvements are inherently difficult to achieve. It seems likely, therefore, that it will be just as difficult in the future as it has been in the

165

past to improve productivity in the bus industry, and we can only assume that the rate of improvement will continue to be at a modest level of 0·5—1·5 per cent a year. If the subsidy to the industry does not increase, then prices will continue to rise relative to the average rise in prices throughout the rest of the economy.

All this may seem a long way from autotram, but it shows that while automation may at the moment represent only a marginal improvement over human operation, it heralds the possibility of continuous future improvements in the cost of vehicles, the cost of control, and the cost of track construction.

In summary, it seems that there are grounds on both sides of the cost—benefit equation for expecting the position of autotram to improve *vis-à-vis* bus operation. Improvements in science and technology will favour transport systems with a low labour content, since these will be more easily able to absorb these improvements. Viewing this in a broader perspective, these improvements will lead to a higher standard of living where it appears that people place a high value (in terms of money) on leisure time.

The comparison with rail

The other main form of public transport in British towns today is the railway based on the standard rail gauge of 4ft. 8½in. (1·435m), the tram having for all practical purposes disappeared. It occurs in a number of forms, including suburban rail, where the track is shared with long-distance passenger and goods trains, and the metros (including the London Underground), where the track is not shared. The feature of these systems that is most relevant in the present context is the high capital cost of their track (£1—3 million), and the large vehicles (with more than 200 places), and large cross-section involved. The cost (per passenger km) tends to be similar to that for a bus if no account is taken of the original cost of track, but trains are considerably faster than buses (by more than 25km per hour). The advantage in speed, though clear-cut if we compare actual installations, is misleading. Rail-based systems rarely provide a comprehensive transport service along a corridor. Station spacings tend to be greater than 1km, and the service is often designed to provide a fast journey from the suburbs to the city centre, where station spacing may be lower. This is true of both the London suburban rail system and the Underground, though the latter offers a slightly less extreme example. The fact that the rule need not always apply, however, is demonstrated by the Paris Métro, where the distance between stations is often as low as 400m.

166

It was argued in Chapter 2 that buses are suited to low and medium levels of passenger demand, whereas reserved-track systems become viable only when passenger demand is high. Autotram cannot compete with bus operation on all-purpose roads at low levels of demand because of the capital cost of the reserved track. Neither is autotram large enough to carry the heavy loads now carried by metros. Its rôle is an intermediate-capacity transport system suited to situations where peak passenger demand is between 4,000 and 10,000 an hour. The lower figure is applicable only where 100 per cent ground-level track is possible; where lengths of overhead track or tunnel are used, demand must be higher. Autotram can be regarded as a small automated railway with a relatively low capital cost. This makes it viable in situations where the larger rail-based systems, with their high track costs, are not. The dividing line between autotram and an automated railway (such as the Victoria Line in London or BARTD in San Francisco were intended to be) is an arbitrary division based on size rather than on operating philosophy.

So far the discussion has been based on a comparison between autotram and buses and, to a lesser extent, railways. This represents the situation in the UK, but it does not take account of the modern tramways that have been developed in Europe. Not only are there a large number of tram systems operating in Europe, but there are also a number of systems, often referred to as 'pre-metro', in which the vehicles are similar in size to trams, but use segregated tracks where they pass through congested areas. Trams may therefore not only be superior to buses under certain demand conditions, but may also represent a more attractive alternative than automated vehicle systems. Will the existence of reserved-track tram systems in many European cities inhibit or encourage the adoption of automation when the benefit of reserved track has already been achieved?

The question cannot be answered by comparing the change in costs from automating an existing tram system (or the change in costs suffered by using drivers on autotram vehicles), because other variables, especially vehicle size, are dependent on the existence or otherwise of automation. If automation is justified, then the argument will not be just an assessment of the worth of taking the drivers off the vehicles and replacing them with perhaps cheaper black boxes and trackside computers to assist the passage of vehicles. It is also necessary to take account of the tendency, found in most automated schemes, but not so pronounced in asynchronous control schemes for instance, to transfer costs from vehicles to the trackside; and a decision must be made on whether this encourages the use of smaller

167

vehicles. If it does, then the increased frequency of vehicles must be counted as a benefit, an improvement that is probably more important in the off-peak than in the peak period, when frequency will usually be high. The arguments in favour of automation are likely to be stronger where the trams operate entirely on a reserved track, rather than where they operate partially along roads and new track construction is needed.

Economics: other towns

How large is the market for an intermediate capacity transport system such as autotram?

In the Coventry study, we found that the improved service offered by autotram for a fare level just covering operating costs yielded a substantial benefit to passengers. The rate of return was just under 10 per cent, meaning that the project was on the margin of acceptability using economic criteria. Where might we expect to find conditions more favourable to the introduction of autotram? These would occur where the capital costs per km were less, the density of passenger demand greater, or both.

In Coventry, over 60 per cent of the track was at ground level. Only in cases where it is possible for the proportion to be higher will the capital costs per km be less. We are likely to encounter this only when there is already an available right of way (for instance, a railway route) or when there is a 'green fields' site available (such as may occur in the case of substantial redevelopment or in the design of a new town).

The higher the passenger demand, the higher the level of benefits offered by an autotram route and the greater the chance that these will exceed the fixed capital cost. With capital costs as found in Coventry, a peak passenger demand of 5,790 people per hour is nearly adequate for economic success. Only in towns with a population of over 300,000 are we likely to find corridors that will guarantee a level of passenger demand higher than 6,000 per hour.

Whether these routes yield an acceptably high rate of return also depends on the capital cost of track through the corridor. This conclusion is dependent on the stability of a number of relationships found in the original Coventry study. For instance, a change in the ratio of peak demand to all-day demand, or the existence of a very poor alternative public transport (due perhaps to very bad road conditions), may alter the balance of advantage.

Particularly relevant to the economic position of autotram in the future is the trend in the total demand for public transport in urban areas. The trend in the last 20 years offers little comfort to autotram; but the growing realisation in recent years that the past trends in car ownership and use cannot continue in the future is likely to favour public transport. Although the exact results of this recent change in public policy are difficult to forecast, it could lead to a stable, and probably an increasing, demand for public transport. For autotram this change is doubly important: not only does it suggest a steady, and perhaps buoyant, market for public transport, but it is also likely to encourage demand in areas that are favourable to autotram. The capacity of the road system in the centre of our larger cities has almost, if not actually, been reached, and, as extra (and in some cases existing) car use is discouraged, demand for public transport on the radial routes serving the centres of these cities will tend to increase. It is this type of demand that autotram is most suited to serve.

One feature of autotram that will undoubtedly inhibit its adoption in some cities is its inflexibility: once the track is built, the major part of the cost cannot be recovered. If demand does not come up to expectations, or costs are higher than anticipated, then the opportunity for adjustments is limited. Mistakes must be lived with; and in this respect autotram, and all-reserved track systems, are at a disadvantage compared with the bus. Bus routes can be altered and schedules adjusted to changes in circumstances; mistakes can be quickly rectified — even surplus buses have a respectable second-hand value (and their cost of removal is very small). Considerations such as these are likely to be taken in account by politicians and decision-makers before they commit substantial funds to autotram. The tendency will be to defer decisions or attempt to keep irreversible commitments to a minimum, except in cases where the change promises substantial benefits.

Environment: other towns

In the study of Coventry it was shown that autotram can offer a convenient service to the public without excessively disturbing other activities and sources of enjoyment, and without large-scale redevelopment. This is possible because of its ability to negotiate sharp curves and steep gradients. On the other hand, it does not seem that autotram can be built along urban streets without seriously disturbing other activities in the street or adversely affecting their appearance. Autotram is not more beautiful than a conventional railway, but is easier to hide away. All towns contain land of low economic value: land alongside railway tracks,

169

derelict land, and land sterilised by poor access to the road network. Towns also contain suburban areas awaiting development, and new activity patterns can here be planned from scratch.

The Coventry study revealed three kinds of area posing different problems for autotram track placed in streets:

(1)   areas of high residential density associated with the area of the town developed before 1918;
(2)   areas of low residential density developed since 1918;
(3)   the central area: an area of largely business activity developed at high densities.

In areas of high residential density, autotram could not be built along existing streets because of elementary public-health constraints. In low density areas, streets are wider, the same public-health restrictions do not apply, and ground-level or elevated track might be accommodated; nevertheless, in the case of Coventry, a sacrifice in road capacity would be unavoidable, and massive overhead structures would be out of scale with the surrounding development. In central areas the problems of severance are likely to rule out ground-level track: pedestrian density is high and random crossing of streets common (and encouraged in pedestrian precincts). Overhead track is usually easier to accommodate in central areas owing to the absence of residential buildings with their stiff public health constraints. However, in most central areas (except perhaps the most modern) it would still result in the insertion of structures which are both large and unacceptable in relation to their surroundings. In Coventry, with a city centre largely rebuilt since the war, it might be possible to insert the track at about the roof level of buildings (there is a uniform roof height over much of the central area).

A few years ago it was thought that redevelopment — often described as 'urban renewal' — would ease the introduction of automatic transport into central areas; but large-scale urban renewal is an expensive operation. It cannot be justified purely as a way to improve transport, but, if large areas of towns were to be redeveloped anyway, to replace housing or make better use of commercial areas, then the introduction of a reserved-track system could be achieved at minimum economic and environmental cost.

It was by exploiting such opportunities that the Buchanan Report hoped to improve the access of private cars to central areas.[2] Eight years later, a working party set up by Westminster City Council saw the redevelopment of large areas of central London as providing an opportunity for the introduction of an autotram system. Buchanan's suggestion that the redevelopment of Oxford Street could be used to improve car access was mirrored eight years later by proposals to use the redevelopment of Regent Street to construct an autotram route between Oxford Circus and Piccadilly Circus.[3] In fact, urban renewal has never materialised in the manner anticipated by the transport planners of the 1960s. It has proved impossible to co-ordinate redevelopment proposals, even on adjacent sites, so as to create transport corridors between them. In addition, there is growing resistance to wholesale changes — involving the destruction of familiar places and landmarks — in the appearance of towns. Public authorities are now more wary of the benefits of 'comprehensive redevelopment', and it is unrealistic to assume that redevelopment will play a significant part in the future planning of autotram routes in central areas. It should be emphasised, however, that it is only central-area redevelopment that has failed to materialise in the manner originally expected. In the suburbs, housing redevelopment is still widespread, and large areas of land lie fallow for several years. This type of redevelopment still offers opportunities for autotram, and was made use of in the Coventry study.

It is unwise to base conclusions too heavily on the experience of one town, and it is useful to speculate on whether the physical conditions in Coventry are likely to be repeated in other towns. Two factors had an important influence on the choice of routes in Coventry:

(1)   the availability of railway land and areas of comprehensive suburban redevelopment;
(2)   the narrowness of the radial roads — a factor inhibiting their use as rights of way for autotram.

There is no reason to believe that Coventry is particularly well endowed with either railway land or comprehensive redevelopment areas. Coventry was never a major railway junction: it now contains one main trunk passenger and goods route and two branch lines. Many towns of similar size contain more rail rights of way, in use or abandoned. There has been less wholesale clearance of old suburbs than in other towns (particularly the conurbations), because Coventry enjoyed a different development cycle. Its most rapid growth was after 1870, when public-health legislation began to improve the standard of house building.

Many towns possess wider radial roads than Coventry does (maximum 25m between property lines), and in addition have more dual carriageways. Some urban areas also contain old tram rights of way. In Leeds and Liverpool, for example, many central reservations could be used for either ground-level or elevated autotram routes.

It is difficult to anticipate public reaction to new structures in towns.

Road plans drawn up ten years ago for large cities reveal how inadequately administrators and planners then appreciated the way people would react to a radical programme of construction. This is not to accuse the planners and engineers of being unfeeling or philistine. In the UK in 1960, the urban motorway was a new phenomenon, and until some were actually built it was difficult to assess how people would react to them. Once their impact had been seen, there was a strong adverse reaction, which led to a more sympathetic view being taken of environmental complaints.

The same observations hold true for the introduction of autotram, though we certainly possess more information about people's attitudes towards environmental issues now than we did ten years ago. It is clear that people are unlikely to tolerate substantial programmes for redeveloping cities in the interests of autotram unless the policies concerned will produce clear benefits.

Notes

[1] *Annual Summary of Accounts and Statistical Information,* Association of Public Passenger Transport Operators, 1973.
[2] *Traffic in Towns,* HMSO, 1963.
[3] Westminster City Council, *An Aid to Pedestrian Movement,* 1971.

10 The Development of Automated Transport and the Process of Innovation

The definition of innovation suggested by the Central Advisory Council on Science and Technology is 'the technical, industrial and commercial steps which lead to the marketing of new manufactured products and to the commercial use of new technical processes and equipment'.[1] At the risk of oversimplification, we can say the process of innovation lies between those of invention and diffusion. Invention is when the feasibility of a new product or new production process is established or even just postulated; and diffusion, which follows innovation, is the process during which the new product (or method) is adopted by more and more organisations or people. The successful management of innovation lies in matching the ever-changing requirements of society and the technical possibilities generated by the inventor.

This chapter examines the process of innovation in the area of automated transport, with particular reference to the UK. It reviews the progress so far (to December 1974) and discusses the rôle played by central government and the prospects for the future.

Automated transport in the UK

Interest in automated transport in the UK was first sparked off by a paper read to the Annual Meeting of the Institution of Mechanical Engineers by L.R. Blake on 28 October 1966.[2]

> The proposed system is an automatic-taxi, public-transport service for towns and cities, capable of 10,000 passengers per hour per track and aimed to be competitive with the private car.
>
> Mini-sized cars are used which carry up to four adult passengers, using induction-motor drives powered from an overhead rail. The cars are driverless and route themselves at 35 mile/h to their destination with no stops at intermediate stations, though they are

Fig. 10.1   Impression of a tubeway in an existing town, changing direction at a crossroads
Source: Report by L.R. Blake, Institution of Mechanical Engineers, 1966

slowed down when changing to another line. The cars move along a lightweight totally-enclosed track of less than 7ft diameter, which can be supported above existing roadways or buildings. [See also Fig. 10.1.]

Although the technical details suggested in Blake's paper have not been adopted by any developers, the concept, described in the paper, of an automated taxi service still retains its original form. It represented then, and continues to represent, the ideal public transport service, provided the technical and environmental details of its construction and operation can be overcome at an acceptable economic cost. It describes a summit of public transport provision, both a target to aim for and an ideal to be compared with existing public transport.

Early in 1967, Brush Electrical Engineering Co. Ltd (L.R. Blake's employer, a subsidiary of Hawker Siddeley Ltd) and the National Research and Development Corporation (NRDC) set up a joint company, Autotaxi Developments Ltd, to promote and carry out design studies on the proposed system. The Joint Transport Research Committee of the

Ministry of Transport and the Ministry of Technology also took an interest in the project and, through their Transport Research Assessment Group (TRAG), asked the Royal Aircraft Establishment (RAE) at Farnborough to carry out a series of technical and economic feasibility studies on the subject. These were referred to as 'Cabtrack' studies, and a major report[3] was published in December 1968, after nine months of detailed study. (The report was not released for public consumption for another three years.) Summarising the findings of the study, the report noted that 'at present the results look encouraging both on technical and economic grounds' (p. 197). It was less certain on the subject of the environment: 'whether the [overhead structure]. . . would be acceptable to architects, town planners, and the public is a field for further study' (p. 199). Further work was undertaken to investigate and confirm these preliminary findings, and to carry out more detailed design studies. In addition, TRAG commissioned a study by a firm of consultant architects (Robert Matthew, Johnson-Marshall and Partners), their brief being to suggest designs for some system components (track, stations and vehicles), to estimate the cost of the structure, and, most important, to assess the environmental effects of a Cabtrack installation.

By 1970, a battery-powered test vehicle was running on a 200m loop of track to test the cab suspension and switching systems. A one-fifth scale track and ten vehicles with computer control were also under construction.

1971 seems to have been a watershed in the history of Cabtrack (autotaxi) in the UK. TRAG, which had been sponsoring the work at the RAE, was now part of the Road Research Laboratory (now the Transport and Road Research Laboratory) in the Ministry of Transport (now Department of the Environment). The Annual Report of the RRL for 1971 reported that 'during 1971 the study has been directed towards systems like Minitram using larger vehicles in a shared mode, as these appear to be more suitable for the initial installations, which are likely to be in relatively small areas which do not justify the full sophistication of a network cab system'.[4] It appears that TRAG felt that initial installations of Cabtrack were, for economic reasons, likely to be modest. They would probably be in a city centre, where journey lengths are small and the advantage of non-stop journeys much diminished. A Minitram scheme might therefore be the better system to install in this limited area, although, as the network expanded, Cabtrack would eventually become the 'best' option. The possibility of Minitram as a stepping stone to the more sophisticated Cabtrack concept was expressed even more forcefully in a report prepared under contract to TRAG (though, with the usual civil-service reticence, the report declares that the views expressed there are not necessarily the views of the DOE or the TRRL — a method of sharing in the praise and avoiding the responsibility for mistakes):

> If a small installation is successful, can it be expanded to the full Cabtrack concept without starting all over again? There is no technical reason why this cannot be done. The initial installation need not have all the properties of the full system. Much of the control technology can be common to Cabtrack and Minitram, and the curvature, headroom and intersection of a guideway structure capable of taking the higher capacity Minitram vehicles are certainly appropriate for cabs.
>
> The relevance of modern Minitram developments is that it is highly compatible with the network cab concept. . . .[5]

The association between Minitram and Cabtrack is today not seen to be so close — certainly, there have been no later official references to the desirability of designing track and control technology for Minitram with the eventual evolution of Cabtrack in mind. In a later report[6] examining a potential Minitram route in Sheffield, there is no mention of keeping track or control-system design flexible in order to cater for Cabtrack (in fact, there is no mention of Cabtrack at all). The close association seems to have been almost, if not actually, a demonstration of faith in Cabtrack and an unwillingness to drop a line of inquiry that had been followed for almost five years. We shall come back to this problem of 'changing direction' later in the chapter.

There were undoubtedly other, and perhaps stronger, reasons for a redirection of development away from Cabtrack. A summary of the consultants' report on the environmental implications of Cabtrack was published in the *Architects' Journal* (19 May 1971). Although the report, which examines an area of central London as an example of a potential candidate for Cabtrack, was optimistic ('the final network could in our view result in a net improvement in the living conditions of the area we have studied'), the professional reaction of planners and architects was hostile. There seems little doubt that this led to a reappraisal of the ease and speed with which automated systems using elevated structures might be introduced in the UK. No doubts about Cabtrack's economic viability seem to have arisen at this time: rates of return were expected to be 'probably between 8 and 12 per cent for the system . . . up to 20 per cent if cab sharing was used to increase occupancy at peak periods'.[7] Whether serious problems had arisen on the technical side we do not know, but it is probable that a long period of development was anticipated and that

176

Minitram, with its shorter gestation period, was thought preferable.

When official interest turned from Cabtrack to Minitram, the prospects for the latter did not look promising. The Advanced Systems Division (or TRAG, as it then was) had assisted the City of Westminster in a study of the transport possibilities in the redevelopment of the Covent Garden site in Central London. The system studied was Minitram, and the conclusions were unenthusiastic.[8] The report admitted that the comprehensive building redevelopment taking place in the City of Westminster provided a unique opportunity for trying out a new mode of transport that would undoubtedly bring benefits to travellers; but Minitram's financial viability could not be demonstrated and the preferred route for the system needed to leave the redevelopment area, thus raising environmental problems in existing parts of the town: 'To impose any new system then will be much more difficult, much more expensive, and perhaps not possible.'[9]

The results of the reappraisal carried out by TRAG during 1971 and 1972 became public in April 1973. In a paper [10] given at TRRL by the head of the Advanced Systems Division, a programme for the development of Minitram was outlined. There was to be no crash programme. A £10–16 million programme was to culminate, it was hoped, in a public demonstration project in Sheffield (population 570,000) around 1980.

The programme began with two competitive feasibility and project-definition studies, which were eventually completed in September 1974. The project-definition studies examined the technical feasibility and demonstration problems of Minitram vehicles and new control systems. Two contracts were let: one to Hawker Siddeley Dynamics, which had taken over the earlier work of Brush Electrical Engineering Co. (both firms are subsidiaries of Hawker Siddeley Ltd), and the other to Easams Ltd, a subsidiary of GEC Ltd. Concurrent with these two technical studies, the firm of consultants that had undertaken the earlier London study carried out a study examining the civil-engineering and architectural implications of a 2·4km line in central Sheffield.[6] This study was carried out without any commitment either to the DOE or Sheffield Council, but it was hoped that it would provide the basis on which a public demonstration project might be founded. The technical studies were carried out on a competitive basis, and the successful contractor is expected to be responsible for the development of Minitram vehicles and their control system for Sheffield. This development is expected to be complete before the commencement of the demonstration project, the purpose of which is essentially to answer questions of public acceptance: people's reaction to automated vehicles and overhead track, the ability of the system to cater for the disabled, and so on. The cost of the programme is expected to be £2–4 million for the Minitram development and £8–12 million for the demonstration project.

The programme reflects a cautious approach to the introduction of Minitram, a recognition of the fact that there are still some important technical problems to be overcome, an appreciation of the difficulty of installing overhead structures in British cities, and an assumption that the advantages of Minitram are not so great at the present time as to justify any expensive crash programme.

One important constraint on the time scale of the programme for a demonstration project in Sheffield is the parliamentary timetable. Legal authority to construct a Minitram line in Sheffield requires the passing of a private parliamentary bill for the construction of a tramway. Mainly as a result of the rigidity of the parliamentary timetable in dealing with such matters, this process is expected to take up to a year.[11]

There remains the possibility that the demonstration project in Sheffield – if it comes to fruition – will not be the first Minitram installation in the UK. Not only do Sheffield District Council, together with the South Yorkshire Passenger Transport Authority, still retain the power of veto over the project,[12] but there is a strong possibility that a route presenting fewer environmental and legal problems may be found elsewhere in the UK. An abandoned railway track may provide this opportunity.

In the admittedly short history of automated transport in the UK (from the time of Blake's paper in 1966 to 1974), two notable features stand out. First, the rôle of government has been crucial: without government encouragement and financial backing, it is unlikely that any significant work in this area would have been carried out. Only one company (Hawker Siddeley and its subsidiaries) has carried out serious commercial development in the area, its efforts including an unsuccessful bid for a project in Ontario, Canada. Easams has been involved only during the Sheffield project-definition study of 1973–74. Of the total expenditure on R & D in automated transport, probably over 75 per cent has been financed by government, either directly or through contract work. (We have included the NRDC in 'government', since, although it is an independent body, it is financed by government specifically to encourage new products and processes.) A second feature of this period has been the changing view of automated transport. This is not well documented; but it is possible, with careful reading of official statements, to detect shifts in emphasis and opinions – the most notable being the change in stress from Cabtrack to Minitram. We shall argue later that changes in direction are to be expected and almost inevitable during the introduction of new technology.

178

Automated transport developments in the USA

Most activity, if not progress, in the field of automated transport has taken place in the USA. During the first half of the 1960s, two important developments were taking place. W.H. Alden was developing a concept of dual-mode vehicles: small vehicles designed to be capable of travelling both on normal roads and on a reserved track under automatic control. The concept eventually evolved into an autotaxi system with the vehicles confined to a reserved track; and this system, known as the Alden Starrcar, was used as a basis for the Morgantown system. At the same time, the giant Westinghouse Corporation was developing the Transit Expressway or Skybus system, and in 1965 a loop of track was opened in South Park, near Pittsburgh. Whether this installation can claim to be the first autotram installation is a contentious point. Certainly the vehicles were, and still are, fully automated, but the size of the vehicles (width 2·6m) is on the edge of, or slightly outside, the definition of autotram. Since 1965, Westinghouse has had only limited success in its attempts to find alternative areas of application for Skybus: two airport installations have been built (at Tampa and Sea-Tac) and another (Miami) is under construction, but so far there are no urban installations, even though there were protracted discussions about the possibility of introducing the system in Pittsburgh.

Concern with the problems of urban transport prompted Congress to amend the Urban Mass Transportation Act of 1964, placing greater emphasis on an examination of possible new technical developments. The relevant part of the legislation read as follows:

> The Secretary [of the Department of Housing and Urban Development] shall undertake a project to study and prepare a program of research, development, and demonstration of new systems of urban transportation that will carry people and goods within metropolitan areas speedily, safely, without polluting the air, and in a manner that will contribute to sound city planning. The program shall (a) concern itself with all aspects of new systems of urban transportation for metropolitan areas of various sizes including technological, financial, economic, governmental and social aspects; (b) take into account the most advanced technologies and materials; and (c) provide national leadership to efforts of States, localities, private industries, universities, and foundations.

In the years 1967–68, the Department of Housing and Urban Development (HUD) awarded a total of 17 contracts to a wide variety of organisations. A Stanford Research Institute report[13] 'of ideal tech-nological futuristic solutions to urban transportation problems, solutions available in from five to ten years' exuded optimism: 'benefits from the use of such systems would amply justify the cost of their development, installation and operation . . . the prospective benefits are so great that the R&D program should be initiated as quickly as possible . . .'. Another report,[14] by the General Research Corporation, concluded that 'increased investment in conventional transit is not likely to arrest the persistent patronage decline that plagues public transit . . . and that any real hope for maintaining and improving transit attractiveness rests with the new systems of personal and dual mode transit'. Although these reports were not followed by an immediate surge in government funding for automated transport, there has been a steady, but unspectacular, increase since then.

Three important components of the United States' R&D programme were: a demonstration of potential systems at the Transpo '72 exhibition; an installation at Dallas/Fort Worth Airport in Texas; and an ill-fated demonstration project at Morgantown, West Virginia.

At the Transpo '72 exhibition, four manufacturers (Ford, Rohr, Bendix-Dashaveyor, and TTI-Otis), partly financed by the Department of Transportation, built short test tracks, and the public were allowed to use the vehicles running along them.

At Dallas/Fort Worth airport, the Airtrans system developed by Ling Temco Vought (LTV) Aerospace went into passenger-carrying service at the beginning of 1974. It is 20 km in length and provides transport between several airport buildings and car parks. The system comprises a complex set of routes, with large autotram vehicles operating according to fixed schedules.

The project at Morgantown connects the town centre with various parts of the university. The vehicles, though large (21 passengers), provide a non-stop journey between the three stations on the network. Originally expected to open for passenger service in 1973, the system is now hoped to be in operation in mid-1975. Cost estimates for the 6·4km system have escalated from $13·5 million in 1970 to $64 million in 1974.

Activity in the USA has been running at a consistently high level (as compared with the UK at least) during the past six to seven years. This is reflected not only in the level of federal funding, but also in the number of organisations seriously developing automated systems (ten such manufacturers are listed in the Appendix), the number of installations now in existence (these range from the simple automatic shuttle systems found in many airports to more sophisticated ones, such as the system in Morgantown), and the number of studies being undertaken of possible installations. Private industry also seems to have shown more interest and initiative than its counterpart in the UK has. Government funds have certainly encouraged development, but there is little doubt that firms such as Westinghouse, LTV and Boeing would have continued development – albeit at a reduced rate of spending – without government backing. The difference between American and British private-sector initiative in the field of new technology is not confined to transport, and concern has often been expressed at the excessive concentration of R&D resources in the public sector in the UK. [15]

The absence of good public transport in the USA is one important reason why greater effort is taken there than in the UK and other countries in Europe to develop automated transport. Whereas the number of public transport trips per capita per year in most European cities exceeds 200, it is rare to find a city in the USA where it exceeds 150, and it is often less than 100. The higher level of demand, together with the higher densities, of European cities has ensured at least a basic public transport system there. In addition, the higher average income in the USA tends to favour transport systems providing a higher quality of service.

European and Japanese developments

Outside the UK and USA, the only countries actively developing automated transport are Germany, France and Japan. In the late 1960s, three German organisations – Krauss-Maffei AG, Siemens, and a consortium comprised of Messerschmitt-Bölkow-Blohm and Demag – started serious development work. Krauss-Maffei concentrated on an autotram system – Transurban TAKT – employing electromagnetic levitation. The firm was awarded a contract by the Province of Ontario, Canada, for installation of a demonstration system at the Canadian National Exhibition grounds in Toronto, where it is expected the system will be operational in the summer of 1975. The MBB-Demag consortium, which is developing an autotaxi system, has a 300m test track in operation at Hagen in the Ruhr. Siemens is developing a suspended system, which could evolve as a variant of either autotaxi or autotram.

At least two organisations in France (Matra Engins and Compagnie d'Énergetique Linéare) are seriously developing automated transport systems. Matra Engins is the more prominent, with two systems – Aramis and VAL – that represent the ends of the service spectrum in automated transport.

Japanese developers have been particularly active in recent years, and six companies appear to be involved in the field. These are: Kawasaki Heavy Industries Ltd (with their KCV system), Mitsubishi Heavy Industries Ltd (MAT), Mitsui and Co. Ltd (VONA), Toshiba Electric Co. Ltd (Mini-Monorail), Hitachi Ltd (Paratran), and the Japan Society for Promotion of Machine Industry (CVS, the only Japanese autotaxi development).

In all three countries, government backing has been heavy, and, although no firm figures showing total expenditure or the breakdown into government and private finance are available, there is little doubt that at least 75 per cent of expenditure has been financed by central government. There is also little doubt that total expenditure in these countries is running at a rate higher than in the UK, but lower than in the USA. Notably, each of the three countries is still developing at least one autotaxi system, though there appears to be greater emphasis on autotram.

Throughout the world, the development of automated systems is almost entirely restricted to large organisations. Although an individual (for instance, L.R. Blake or W.H. Alden) may initiate a new idea and even carry out some of the early development, the heavy cost of R&D, together with the complexity of any fully automated transport system, has made it inevitable that organisations with more substantial resources (financial and manpower) should take over or absorb the development at some stage. It is also interesting to note that these organisations have a wide variety of backgrounds, and that often they have limited or no experience of urban transport. All, however, have experience of mechanical or electrical engineering, in such fields as computers, aerospace, lifts and cranes.

Public policy

The aim of public policy is to identify the gap between where society is, or where it is going, and where it ought to go; and then to attempt by the means at its disposal to steer society in the required direction. The government may feel that its rôle is merely to create a favourable environment in which private individuals and organisations may prosper, but under other circumstances it may feel that more energetic promotion or interference is needed. Technical innovation is one such area. The argument usually advanced to justify government initiative in promoting new technology is based on the tendency for private industry to underinvest in research and development. Three reasons are proposed to explain this tendency. First and foremost, R&D is a risky adventure: great gains may accrue, but, on the other hand, large losses may be incurred. Society may feel that the risk is worthwhile, that in the long run the gains will balance the losses, but for the private firm a loss may spell ruin. It is thus argued that firms will generally tend to play safe on speculative ventures, especially when R&D costs are large relative to the firm's resources – as often happens today with modern technology increasing in complexity all the time.

A second difficulty associated with firms operating in a capitalist system, where success is judged at least in part in terms of financial gain, is that of inappropriability. The patent system, which evolved to protect the inventor or the innovator and to allow him to appropriate the financial benefits resulting from his invention, can less easily protect property rights attendant on advances in modern technology, especially where concerned with processes.

A third reason why industrial firms may be deterred from the energetic pursuit of R&D is the limited relevance that many of the results may have to the firm in question as opposed to the society of which it is part. Firms often prove hesitant when lines of inquiry are likely to lead to products or services outside their usual line of business. This tendency is likely to be more prevalent in small firms, and in firms where the necessary expertise for diversion is non-existent or difficult to find.

All five of the countries involved in the development of automated transport have accepted the force of these arguments. Not only are their governments active in encouraging R&D, but they also, to varying degrees, maintain some control over the course of development. Naturally, any use to which grants or subsidies from the public exchequer are put by private industry needs to be monitored in the interests of the taxpayer; but the government may also feel that it has more experience and knowledge about urban transport than the firms carrying out the R&D. This is undoubtedly true in automated transport, where the majority of developers have little previous experience of urban transport problems. The central government, with its long experience of analysing urban problems and forming public policy, is then in an ideal position to represent the needs of the consumer to the developer. This rôle may also be carried out by local urban authorities, but, while the central government is still providing substantial funds, it is unlikely that full responsibility would be left in local hands.

Another reason for government control is that this would help avoid duplication and waste. A co-ordinated programme of R&D can avoid the situation where two manufacturers follow the same line of development and come to the same conclusion at twice the cost. Central government agencies must exercise considerable skill if they are to prepare a balanced programme of R&D and make the most fair and suitable choice of organisations to carry it out.

One criticism often levelled against the promoters of new technology is their failure to take account, in the early stages of development, of customers' needs. Developers tend to follow rather simple lines of improvement — such as making something faster or bigger — with little reference to factors such as cost or environment. Later, when the force of these objections becomes known, it may be necessary to make expensive readjustments to the development programme, or the substantial funds already invested in the project may make it difficult to abandon. The development of supersonic aircraft, such as Concorde, exhibits some, or perhaps all, of these features. In the early stages of the development of automated transport, the charge that too much emphasis was being placed on technical novelties, and not enough on the economics of the exercise and the environmental impact of the systems, may have been correct. But the charge would be more difficult to substantiate today. A major part of the development programme in the UK is concerned with the environmental impact of overhead structures, and there is no reason to believe that other countries are any less aware of the impact these structures might have on their urban areas. Authoritative papers or statements on the economics of automated systems are less forthcoming, but the papers that do exist leave no doubt that the proposed systems are more expensive than conventional public transport.

The course of policy

Criticism of public policy towards innovation in automated transport (and in all areas of innovation) is in one sense easy, yet in reality difficult. Such things as the pursuit of unfruitful lines of inquiry, the failure to pursue the more profitable lines, and frequent changes in attitude or emphasis all provide excuses for criticism. But, to be fair to decision-makers, any criticisms should be made in the light of the information available to them at the time the decision was made. Good decisions *ex ante* may turn out to be the wrong ones *ex post*, and *vice versa*. [16] We must recognise that innovation is a complex process, in which goals may be changed or modified, and in which the path to a goal is, by definition, unknown and uncharted. The impression that the path from invention to consumer use — defined here as the path of innovation — is as certain and as well documented as a footpath on a map is a travesty of reality. Innovation is

184

the search for and confirmation of new knowledge. There is no well-trodden path to follow, for innovation is an attempt to find a path that will eventually lead to the destination. As development proceeds, new facts are learnt: facts about technology (for instance, process A is better than process B, and metal X is not hard enough); facts about people's values (people protest strongly when G is imposed on them, but enthuse over the new product X); and facts outside the control of the developer (Mr Y has invented a new metal, and Mr Z can now produce this machine more cheaply). To pretend that a blueprint for success − an infallible critical-path diagram − is available invites failure and despair. Perhaps worse, new information that calls for a change in direction will be bitterly contested or ignored, to save face. Pride will insist that, where a change in direction is unavoidable, it should be camouflaged and stretched out over a long period of time − both factors contributing to confusion and delay. At the outset it should be recognised that changes in direction will need to be made; mistakes can then be quickly and painlessly identified and a new course steered without recriminations.

A corollary to this attitude towards new technology is the allocation of resources to projects that are *expected to* fail. It may be quite logical and sensible to spend time and money on long shots − projects that have a small chance of success, but, if they do succeed, pay off handsomely. The one project in ten that pays off justifies the attitude that led to the nine failures.

Once the decision to innovate has been made, the responsible organisation, whether it be commercial or public, must also decide on the level of resources to be allocated to the project. There is little doubt that the scale of effort should be related to the expected returns (either in terms of profit or social benefits). Similarly, it can be expected that, the greater the level of resources devoted to the project, the quicker success can be expected. An attempt to achieve Z by 1990 will almost certainly use less resources than would an attempt to reach it by 1980. The shorter the time available, the greater the tendency to duplicate. When a project is particularly urgent, research in different, but related, areas has to be carried out concurrently and, perhaps, independently. For instance, to take an extreme case, it may be decided that, for reasons of urgency, the suspension, propulsion, guidance and control components of an automated vehicle should be developed concurrently but separately. The design of the suspension, guidance and control must be based on an assumption about the type of propulsion system to be used − say, a linear motor. But, as research continues, the linear motor is modified, or worse still, abandoned and, consequently, the three other areas of research must adapt or reject some of their previous findings, which were justified on the original assumption. In this case a less wasteful, but lengthier, course would have been to carry out at least some of the research into propulsion before committing funds to the other areas. The balance between speed and cost must be decided on the basis of the expected benefits lost by delay in R&D. Early developments in automated transport, especially in the USA, emphasised the former, but recently cost considerations have been more prominent.

A controversial attitude towards innovation in automated transport was expressed by a Parliamentary Committee, which reported in 1972 — 'the UK should study American and German developments closely, but it should not commit substantial funds until the foreign systems have proved themselves in operation'. [17] The danger of this policy to British companies is that they are likely to be at a serious disadvantage when bidding for contracts abroad. Organisations that have built and successfully operated an automated system will find themselves in a much stronger position.

In the case of contracts within the UK, the government may feel that home firms are protected from serious competition either by existing regulations or by the inherent nature of the product or process, where this is such as to make international competition difficult. Even if a contract is awarded to a foreign firm, it is unlikely that all the components will be manufactured abroad. Because of heavy transport charges, the track and vehicle bodies might be produced in the UK, whereas the control system might be produced by the successful contractor in his own country.

If a government wishes to protect and encourage the position of home industry against foreign competition there are numerous measures available to it, all of which have been used in the past. The encouragement given to the European computer industries in the face of American competition bears witness to this. The policy of importing technology was successfully adopted by Japan in the post-war period, but it should be emphasised that in most cases improvements and modifications were made to the original technology.

Notes

[1] *Technological Innovation in Britain,* HMSO, 1968.

[2] L.R. Blake, 'A public transport system using four-passenger, self-routing cars', *Guided Land Transport,* Institution of Mechanical Engineers, Proceedings 1966—67, vol. 181, part 3G.

[3] *Cabtrack Studies. Assessment of Autotaxi Urban Transport Systems,*

Technical Report 68287, Royal Aircraft Establishment, Farnborough, Hants, 1968. There have been a large number of follow-up reports on individual subjects in the period 1969–74.

[4] *Road Research 1971,* HMSO, p. 23.

[5] B.E. Grant, W.J. Russell, *Opportunities in Automated Urban Transport,* 1973; available from Robert Matthew, Johnson-Marshall and Partners, Welwyn Garden City.

[6] *Minitram in Sheffield,* Robert Matthew, Johnson-Marshall and Partners, Welwyn Garden City, 1974.

[7] *Road Research 1971,* HMSO, p. 23.

[8] Westminster City Council, *An Aid to Pedestrian Movement,* 1971.

[9] Ibid., p. 5.

[10] M.H.L. Waters, *Minitram – the TRRL Programme,* Transport and Road Research Laboratory, April 1973.

[11] A. Naysmith, 'The institutional background to Minitram' in I.G. Black *et al., Advanced Transport Systems in British Cities,* Urban Transport Research Group, University of Warwick, 1974.

[12] M.H.L. Waters, op.cit.

[13] Stanford Research Institute, *Future Urban Transportation System: Description, Evaluation and Programs,* 1968.

[14] Summarised in W.F. Hamilton II and D.K. Nance, 'Systems analysis of urban transportation', *Scientific American,* July 1969.

[15] See, for instance, M. Shanks, 'Setting the scene. Five: The United Kingdom', in M. Goldsmith (ed.), *Technological Innovation and the Economy,* Wiley Interscience.

[16] An artificial example may illuminate. Supposing I am asked to guess whether a fair die, when cast, will fall 6 or non-6 (i.e. 1,2,3,4 or 5), then on any sensible criterion I must choose non-6. If, when the die is cast, it falls on the 6, does this devalue the quality of my decision?

[17] *Second Report of the Expenditure Committee on Urban Transport Planning 1972,* HMSO, para. 66.

11 Conclusions, and the Direction of Future Developments

1 Although autotaxis provided the initial impetus for development in automated transport, there is no prospect of their introduction in British cities in the next decade. Not only are there severe technical difficulties to overcome, but the economic and environmental costs of any installation are likely to prove prohibitive.

2 At the other end of the service spectrum, autotram, with its simple line-haul operation and more favourable economics, has a greater chance of being introduced.

3 It is important, when referring to the benefits of autotram, to distinguish between the separate contributions of reserved track, small scale, and automation.

4 Novel forms of suspension (air and magnetic levitation) and linear motors seem to offer no significant improvements over the wheel (rubber tyres or steel wheel) and the rotary electric motor.

5 Simple control techniques based, perhaps, on current railway techniques should prove adequate for autotram operation.

6 Ground-level track offers significant advantages over elevated and underground track: it is both cheaper and environmentally less intrusive. Its main disadvantage is the need for protective fencing and the severance this causes. It would seem that, in most cities, the opportunities for routes based entirely on ground-level track are limited.

7 Elevated track is both expensive and unacceptable in most urban surroundings.

8 Underground track, although slightly more expensive than elevated track, causes no environmental disturbance and offers considerable flexibility in route planning. It might be usefully employed in conjunction with ground-level track. If extensive underground track is used, vehicle design should be closely tailored to the tunnel cross-section.

9 Suspended-vehicle systems suffer the grave disadvantage of not being able to use cheap ground-level track.

10 Compared to the bus, autotram offers a superior service (faster journeys, shorter waiting times), but at greater cost. An autotram route is likely to be justified only at high levels of demand (such as will normally

be found only in towns with a population of at least 300,000), when the capital cost can be shared among many passengers. This conclusion also assumes that it will be possible for a high proportion of track to be laid at ground level.

11   The tendency for the costs of bus operation to rise relative to other prices, and for people's valuation of travelling time to rise in line with incomes, should favour autotram.

12   The immediate benefits of autotram are not great enough to justify a crash R&D programme. Government policy should concentrate on a long-term development programme in the course of which hardware should be developed and further research undertaken into the problems of fitting reserved-track systems into the urban fabric.

Appendix:
Systems under Development

This appendix lists the most prominent developers of automated transport and gives details about nine of the systems that are of particular interest. The nine were chosen not because they were felt to be superior to or more promising than the others, but rather to describe the variety in design and technique that is apparent in automated transport. Other publications (for instance, *Lea Transit Compendium,* which is published twice yearly by N.D. Lea Transportation Research Corporation and describes in detail the automated systems being developed throughout the world) give extensive details of dimensions and performance data. The descriptions given here are intended to convey only the essential characteristics of the systems, and no attempt has been made to delineate all the details, many of which — such as size of vehicle, type of doors, and maximum speed — can be changed to suit particular circumstances.

Fig. A.1 A magnetically levitated autotram: Krauss-Maffei Transurban on its Munich test track
Source: Krauss-Maffei AG, Munich, W. Germany

Fig. A.2   An autotaxi system: rubber tyre support and linear motor propulsion: Demag-MBB Cabinentaxi on its Hagen test track
Source: Demag-MBB, Hagen, W. Germany

Fig. A.3   The guidance mechanism of a Morgantown vehicle: the steering biased to follow the wall on the left hand of the vehicle
Source: Boeing Co., Seattle, USA

Fig. A.4 Air-cushion skirts: the base of an Otis Hovair vehicle
Source: Otis Elevator Co., Denver, Colorado, USA

Fig. A.5 A VAL vehicle: passing the large switch arm on the Lille test track
Source: Engins Matra, Vélizy, France

1	*System name:*	Aramis

Developer: Engins Matra,
37 avenue Louis-Brequet,
78140 Vélizy,
France

Main interests: Engine manufacture

Associated developers: —

Service offered: Personal, on-demand. Vehicles form 'trains' when travelling between stations

Control — path planning: Stochastic

headway: Asynchronous within trains, block between trains

general: —

Method of support: Bottom support in trough track using pneumatic tyres and mechanical spring suspension

Method of propulsion: Rotary electric DC motor

Method of braking: Wheel brakes

Method of guidance: Horizontal wheels bear on the sides of the trough

Method of switching: A vehicle-borne arm embraces the left or right guiderail

Stage of development: 1km test track with three vehicles and one off-line station

Place of development: Orly Airport, Paris, France

2 *System name:*	Cabinentaxi
Developers:	Demag Fördertechnik, D-5800 Hagen, Heinitz Strasse 28, West Germany
	Messerschmitt-Bölkow-Blohm GmbH, D-8000 München 80, Postfach 801265, West Germany
Main interests:	Demag — mechanical and cargo handling equipment, machine tools
	MBB — aerospace manufacture
Associated developers:	—
Service offered:	Personal, on demand
Control — path planning:	Stochastic
headway:	Asynchronous, spacing by three separate non-fail safe systems. Two use signals transmitted via the track, one using direct signal
general:	The overall control is hierarchical. First level — local-section vehicle control. Second level — vehicle demand/supply and switching merges. Third level — optimisation of empty-vehicle despatch. Failure of third level produces reduced efficiency, not shutdown
Method of support:	Vehicles run both above and below a beam using solid rubber tyres
Method of propulsion:	Two linear electric three-phase AC motors
Method of braking:	Separate linear-electric braking motors and wheel drum-brakes
,Method of guidance:	Upper and lower vehicles: horizontal wheels bear on a central spine

Method of switching:	A vehicle-borne arm embraces the left or right guiderail
Stage of development:	300m test track
Place of development:	Hagen, West Germany

3   *System name:*   CVS

Developer:	Japanese Society for the Promotion of Machine Industry, 3-5-8 Shiba Koen, Minato-ku, Tokyo 105, Japan
Main interests:	Development of new products for industrial manufacture and export
Associated developers:	A large number of Japanese firms have combined for this development
Service offered:	Personal, on demand. A dense network mesh with lines spaced at 100m is proposed
Control — path planning:	Deterministic
headway:	Synchronous
general:	The overall control is hierarchical. First level — local computers every 200m. Second level — computer controls routing and local computers. Third level — computer controls $1km^2$ of network. Fourth level — computer controls overall routing and vehicle supply
Method of support:	Bottom support in slotted track using pneumatic tyres and mechanical springs
Method of propulsion:	Rotary electric DC motor
Method of braking:	Air brakes and caliper brakes bearing on a track rail

Method of guidance:	Lateral wheels bear on the sides of the central track slot
Method of switching:	A vehicle-borne arm embraces the left or right guiderail in the central slot
Stage of development:	250m test track, 60 vehicles
Place of development:	Higashi-murayama-shi near Tokyo

4 *System name:* Airtrans

Developer:	LTV Aerospace Corps, Ground Transportation Division, PO Box 5907, Dallas, Texas 75222, USA
Main interests:	Aerospace manufacture
Associated developers:	Texas Bitulithic (track), General Railway Signal Corps (control system)
Service offered:	Shared vehicle, scheduled
Control − path planning:	Stochastic
headway:	Block (vehicle maintained at five-block separation)
general:	Headway is controlled by an independent system. A vehicle computer controls door closing, stopping accuracy. A central computer controls vehicle supply, route planning and switching
Method of support:	Bottom support in trough track using pneumatic (foam-filled) tyres and air-bag suspension
Method of propulsion:	Rotary electric DC motor
Method of braking:	Wheel brakes
Method of guidance:	Lateral wheels bear on the sides of the trough

Method of switching:	A switch blade on the track guides a wheel on the vehicle
Stage of development:	Operational — 20·6km of guideway, 51 passenger vehicles and 17 cargo vehicles
Place of installation:	Dallas/Fort Worth Regional Airport, Texas, USA

5 *System name:*	H-bahn
Developers:	Siemens AG, D-8520 Erlangen, Werner-von-Siemens Strasse 50, West Germany
	Düwag Waggonfabrik Uerdingen AG, D-4000 Düsseldorf, Königsberger Strasse 100, West Germany
Main interests:	Siemens: electrical and electro-mechanical products
	Düwag: railway-vehicle and tram manufacture
Associated developers:	—
Service offered:	Shared vehicle, on demand
Control — path planning:	Deterministic
headway:	Synchronous
general:	Headway control is determined by the synchronous motor drives. Other forms of control are performed by a central computer and its satellites
Method of support:	Suspended from a box-shaped track; internal steel wheels on lower inside face of track support the vehicle
Method of propulsion:	Two linear synchronous electric motors

Method of braking:	Linear motor aided by caliper brakes bearing on a track rail
Method of guidance:	Horizontal steel wheels bear on the sides of the box beam
Method of switching:	The magnetic forces of the two propulsion motors are used to bias the vehicle to the left- or right-hand side of the beam
Stage of development:	1·5km test track
Place of development:	Erlangen, West Germany

6	*System name:*	Hovair
	Developer :	Otis Elevator Co., PO Box 7293, Park Hill Station, Denver, Colorado 80207, USA
	Main interests:	Lift manufacture
	Associated developers :	—
	Service offered:	Shared vehicle, on demand
	Control — path planning :	Deterministic
	headway :	Synchronous
	general :	Overall control is hierarchical. First level — on-vehicle control of speed acceleration and switching. Second level — station control. Third level — headway and merge control. Fourth level — overall vehicle-supply and schedule planning
	Method of support:	Bottom support in trough track using air-cushion suspension
	Method of propulsion :	Single-sided AC three-phase linear induction motor

Method of braking :	Normal — linear motor. Emergency — vehicle drops onto skids
Method of guidance :	Horizontal wheels bear on the sides of the trough
Method of switching :	A vehicle-borne arm embraces the left or right guiderail
Stage of development :	A test track has been in use for five years: demonstration at Transpo '72
Place of development :	Detroit, USA

7   *System name :*   KCV (Kawasaki Computer-Controlled Vehicles)

Developer :	Kawasaki Heavy Industries Ltd, World Trading Center, Hamamatsucho 2-4-1, Minato-ku, Tokyo, Japan
Main interests :	General engineering manufacture
Associated developers :	—
Services offered :	Shared vehicle, scheduled or on demand
Control — path planning :	Stochastic
headway :	Block
general :	A central computer controls the choice of route and all vehicle movements as well as systems checks
Method of support :	Bottom support in trough track using pneumatic (foam-filled) tyres and mechanical springs
Method of propulsion :	Rotary electric motor (whether AC or DC is unknown)
Method of braking :	Wheel brakes
Method of guidance :	Horizontal wheels bear on the side of the trough

201

Method of switching :	Sidewalls are raised or lowered in the switch
Stage of development :	Test track in operation
Place of development :	Not known

8 *System name :* Morgantown

Developer :	The Boeing Co., PO Box 3999, Seattle, Washington 98124, USA
Main interest :	Aerospace manufacture
Associated developers :	Bendix Corp., Alden Self-Transit Systems; sponsored by the US Department of Transportation
Service offered :	Shared vehicle, scheduled in peak periods, on demand at other times
Control — path planning :	Deterministic
headway :	Synchronous
general :	A central computer manages supply of vehicles, route planning and emergency operation; station computers control station movements; vehicle computers control immediate vehicle position and speed relative to synchronous markers
Method of support :	Bottom support in trough track using pneumatic tyres and air-bag suspension. Ackerman steering is used
Method of propulsion :	Rotary electric DC motor
Method of braking :	Wheel brakes
Method of guidance :	The support wheels are biased left or right. A lateral control arm senses the trough wall and alters the steering to permit the vehicle to follow it

202

Method of switching :	The vehicle steering is biased to the left or right wall of the trough at a divergent switch
Stage of development :	A 3·5km system, intended for public use, has been built. This is still (at the end of 1974) under test
Place of development :	Morgantown, West Virginia, USA

9 *System name :*   Transurban (TAKT)

Developer :	Krauss-Maffei AG, D-8000 München 50, Krauss-Maffei Strasse 2, West Germany
Main interests :	Railway locomotive manufacture
Associated developers :	—
Service offered :	Shared vehicle, scheduled
Control — path planning :	Stochastic
headway :	Block
general :	The routing and speed control systems are already in use on some German railways. Schedules and movements are centrally organised, with some functions performed by satellite computers
Method of support :	Bottom-supported by electromagnets attracted to steel rails in the track. The magnetic field strength is regulated by an electronic control system
Method of propulsion :	Single-sided linear AC three-phase induction motor
Method of braking :	Linear motor aided by friction brakes bearing on a track rail
Method of guidance :	The support magnets provide stable lateral guidance

Method of switching :	A second set of electromagnets on board the vehicle selects the path when switched in the correct sequence
Stage of development :	A 1km track is in operation
Place of development :	Munich, West Germany

Other autotaxi systems under development

System name	Developer
Cabtrack	Advanced Systems Division, Transport and Road Research Laboratory, Crowthorne, Berks, UK
Elan-Sig	SIG Swiss Industrial Company, CH-8212 Neuhausen, Rhine Falls, Switzerland
Flyda Chair	Flyda Ltd, The Manor House, South Cerney, Cirencester, Glos., UK
Glide-Ride	Aerial Transit System of Nevada Inc., 3547 Maryland Parkway, Las Vegas, Nevada 89109, USA
Monocab	Monocab Inc. (subsidiary of Rohr Industries Inc.), 2700 Oakland Avenue, Garland, Texas 75401, USA
PRT	Aerospace Corporation, 2350E El Segundo Boulevard, El Segundo, California 90045, USA

Other autotram systems under development

System name	Developer
ACT	Ford Motor Company, Transportation Systems Operation, PO Box 2545, Dearborn, Michigan 48123, USA
Dashaveyor	The Dashaveyor Company (subsidiary of Bendix Corp.), 3300 Plymouth Road, Ann Arbor, Michigan 48107, USA
MAT	Mitsubishi Heavy Industries Ltd, Rolling Stock and Transportation Equipment Division, 501 Marunouchi 2 Chome Chiyoda-ku, Tokyo, Japan
Mini Monorail	Toshiba Electric Co. Ltd, Transportation Division, Uchisara Macho, 100 Chiyoda-ku, Tokyo, Japan
Minirail	Habegger Ltd, Engineering Works, Industriestrasse, Thun, Switzerland
Minitram	Easams Ltd, Elstree Way, Borehamwood, Herts, UK
Minitram	Hawker Siddeley Dynamics Ltd, Manor Road, Hatfield, Herts, UK
Paratran	Hitachi Ltd, 6-2, 2-Chome, Ohtemachi Chiyoda-ku, Tokyo, Japan

Skybus	Westinghouse Electric Corp., Avenue A and West Street, East Pittsburgh, Pennsylvania 15112, USA
Starrcar	Alden Self-Transit Systems Corporation, 64 Sumner Street, Milford, Massachusetts 01757, USA
Tridim	Société de L'Aérotrain, Tour Atlantique, 92 Puteaux, France
Uniflo	Uniflo Systems Company, 7401 Washington Avenue South, Minneapolis, Minnesota 55435, USA
Unitran Monorail	Unitran Monorail Inc., 2207 Border Avenue, Torrance, California 90501, USA
Urba 30	Compagnie d'Énergetiques Linéare, 5 rue Monge, 92 Vanves, France
VAL	Engins Matra, 37 avenue Louis Brequet, 78140 Vélizy, France
VONA	Mitsui and Co. Ltd, 2-9 Nishi Shimbashi, Itchome, Minato-ku, Tokyo, Japan

Index